RUNNING A CHA

NORFOLK COLLEGE
TENNYSON AVENUE KING'S LYNN

RUNNING A CHARITY

Francesca Quint
Barrister

JORDANS
1994

Published by
Jordan Publishing Limited
21 St Thomas Street
Bristol BS1 6JS

British Library Cataloguing-in-Publication Data

A catalogue record for this book is available
from the British Library.

ISBN 0 85308 188 3

361-76 Q

Photoset by Rowland Phototypesetting Limited, Bury St Edmunds, Suffolk
Printed in Great Britain by Henry Ling Limited, The Dorset Press, Dorchester

Foreword

In the foreword to a book on electricity lighting law written in the 1920s, the then Attorney-General wrote that it was a work wherein 'much which was previously obscure is made plain'. I seriously doubted the accuracy of the claim when I used that book. Having read Francesca Quint's book, however, I do believe that such a claim can properly be made for it.

It contains much common sense and should be read by everyone who has the idea of starting a charity, for reading her excellent practical ideas will help them to think about the matters for which they should plan at the outset.

Although some people claim that the Charity Commission is concerned only with investigating errors in charities, it remains one of our main concerns to ensure that what is given to charity is effectively applied to the proper purposes. Even in our investigative mode, we are more concerned with that aspect of matters than any other and we firmly believe that 'prevention is better than cure'.

The advice given in this book is set out in a clear and readable form and will do much to help ensure that investigations are not needed. I therefore warmly welcome its production. I very much hope that it will reach a wide readership and am sure that it will lighten the path of many who are concerned with charity administration.

ROBERT VENABLES
Charity Commissioner
and Head of Legal Staff
Charity Commission
December 1993

Preface

The aim of this book is to provide a general guide for trustees and senior officers of charities to all the major aspects of administering the charity.

Charities have never been more prominent in the perception of the public, and the part they play in almost every aspect of activity within the community continues to grow. There are more charities than ever in existence.

Recently, there has been a considerable upheaval in the relevant legal rules, which has placed more responsibilities on trustees, increased their accountability and strengthened the Charity Commissioners' powers to deal with abuse. At the time of going to press, the Charities Acts 1992 and 1993 are not fully in force. However, there is a timetable for implementation and, for the purposes of this book, I have not differentiated between those parts which are already in force and those which have yet to come into force.

Included in the Appendices are lists of helpful organisations and further reading. These have been drawn from my own experience and are not by any means exhaustive – they are intended to stimulate rather than satisfy the reader's desire for further information.

I would like to express my thanks and admiration for two people who have assisted me by carrying out research and sharing the results. Mrs Una Carlow, BA, Dip TP, who has extensive, hands-on experience of running charities and who is currently Deputy Chief Officer of Swindon and District Community Health Council, has provided considerable assistance on aspects of modern management theory and practice, which I have incorporated into Chapter 4. Sebastian Wilberforce, a solicitor at Messrs Witham Weld of London SW1, has provided the factual basis for Chapter 5 on Europe, in which he takes a special interest. He has also interviewed a number of professional people, whose views have been taken into account in Chapter 4 in the section on 'Dealing with professionals'.

Needless to say, neither Una nor Sebastian is responsible for the interpretation which I have put on their contributions, nor for any errors or omissions – for which I am to blame.

I would also like to thank those professional people who were kind enough to give interviews. They are, in no particular order, Elizabeth Liddell of Charity Solutions; Roy Budgett of TSB Bank plc; John Dale of Kleinwort Benson Charities; Anne Wrangham of Crossbow Research; Nicholas Bellord and Alexa Beale of Witham Weld; Graham Vivian of Chestertons; and Robin

Hill of Clifford Tee & Gale. (Sebastian asked a number of accountants to take part but they were all too busy.)

FRANCESCA QUINT
December 1993

Contents

Chapter 1

INTRODUCTION

What is a charity?

The word 'charity' has a general meaning in ordinary speech and a special meaning in English law. This book is concerned with charity in that special, legal sense.

Since the time of Queen Elizabeth I and before, certain purposes have been regarded by the law as worthy of favourable treatment: the courts and the Charity Commissioners will help to enforce them and prevent abuses through trust law. In addition, the rules which normally require a trust to be brought to an end after a certain length of time ('the perpetuity period') and which restrict the number of trustees, do not apply to charities and, because the purposes are themselves regarded as beneficial to the public, organisations devoted to them are given favourable tax and rating treatment. The courts and the Charity Commissioners also have the power to make a 'scheme' to alter a charity's purposes to bring them up to date or to make them workable.

There is no exhaustive list of charitable purposes, and no strict legal definition of charity, but charitable purposes have been classified as:

1 the relief of poverty;
2 the advancement of education;
3 the advancement of religion; and
4 other purposes beneficial to the community.

Every charitable purpose will come within one (or more) of these four categories, but not every purpose which is within those categories is necessarily charitable. Deciding whether a given purpose is charitable depends on legal precedent and analogy from legal precedent. Sometimes, a purpose which was not regarded as charitable in the past will be accepted as charitable as times change. An example of this is the promotion of racial harmony, which was accepted as a charitable purpose only during the 1980s. The opposite can also occur.

Exclusively charitable purposes

To be a charity, a trust or organisation must be established for exclusively charitable purposes. It is not enough that some of its purposes are charitable if other purposes are commercial, political or for the benefit of private individuals, or even if they are simply good causes which do not come within the legal concept of charity.

As long as the purposes are exclusively charitable it does not matter what form the trust or organisation takes, or what assets it has, or how many people are involved in running it. Charities come in all shapes and sizes. Of course, there are tried and tested forms of trust and organisation and, depending on what the charity aims to achieve, the activities it is involved in and the resources available, there are optimum numbers for the governing body, staff and so on. These matters are discussed in Chapter 2.

Who is a charity trustee?

Charity trustees

The expression 'charity trustees' is defined in the Charities Act 1993 as meaning the body of people responsible for the management and control of the administration of a charity. It can also be termed the charity's 'governing body'. The function of this body, rather than the name given to it, determines whether they are the charity trustees. In this book the expression 'charity trustees' or 'trustees' will be used as a shorthand expression for all those who constitute a charity's governing body, whether they are described as trustees, governors, feoffees, committee members, council members, directors, board members or some other designation. It does not include employees of the governing body, although much of what is said about trustees is directly relevant to the responsibilities of senior staff and officers of a charity.

Some charities have more than one tier of responsibility within their governing structure. For example, the function of holding the legal title to property is often allocated to a body or group of people separate from the decision-makers themselves and (confusingly) the property-holders may be called 'trustees' in the charity's constitution. It is also not uncommon for day-to-day management decisions to be delegated to a small number of the governing body, often called the 'executive committee'.

Anyone who becomes involved in a formal capacity in the running of a charity should be quite clear from the outset whether or not he or she has the responsibilities of a charity trustee. In cases of doubt, the Charity Commissioners or a professional legal adviser will be able to clarify the position.

Responsibilities of charity trustees

A charity trustee shares responsibility with his or her co-trustees. Unless there is a specific provision in the governing instrument requiring a different proportion, decisions are taken on a simple majority vote of those present at a meeting, usually with a casting vote for the chairman of the meeting. All the trustees are bound by a decision properly taken. Attendance at trustees' meetings is, therefore, one of the main duties, and someone whose other commitments do not permit regular attendance should not have a place on the governing body.

Public trust

Trusteeship of a charity is a public trust, which calls for a high degree of integrity. Trusteeship cannot validly be undertaken by a person who is under 18 years of age or who is suffering from mental incapacity. There is no place on a charity's governing body for someone who has an ulterior motive, whether this is political or commercial or a private benefit for the trustee or someone connected with the trustee. It is essential that the governing body are able to satisfy an enquirer that all decisions are taken in good faith in the interests of the charity itself. People who have been convicted of offences involving deception or dishonesty (unless the convictions are spent), or who have been disqualified from acting as company directors or removed involuntarily from previous charity trusteeships cannot become charity trustees and may suffer criminal penalties if they do this. The Charity Commissioners or a professional legal adviser will clarify the situation in case of doubt if given the full facts. In suitable cases the Commissioners are able to waive this restriction.

Conflict

A trustee who stands to gain, however innocently, from a decision of the charity's governing body, or who finds that there is any conflict between his or her duty to the charity and his or her personal interests, should disclose this and take no part in the decision. If the conflict is sufficiently serious or is likely to be prolonged, the trustee concerned may have to avoid attending meetings for a time, or even resign his or her trusteeship. If, however, the trustees as a whole are convinced that the resignation would not be in the charity's interests, they may seek a special dispensation from the Charity Commissioners.

Conflicts can also arise between a trustee's duty to the charity and some other public obligation. This is not uncommon because those who are willing to shoulder responsibilities usually tend to have further responsibilities placed upon them. Charity trustees are often local councillors, school governors or trustees of other charities. Alternatively, trustees may be appointed by outside bodies which have their own interest in the area in which the charity's work lies. If the trustee is appointed by, or a member of, another body, he or she must remember that, as a trustee, his or her duty to the charity overrides all other obligations. If an irreconcilable conflict arises, he or she may have to avoid taking part in decisions of the charity, or attending meetings or, in extreme cases, to resign from one or other position.

Delegation

Trustees must not delegate their responsibilities, except insofar as is permitted by the governing instrument of the charity and by the general law. Thus, trustees take personal responsibility for all major decisions made in their name and, if they allow someone else to decide something on their behalf, they are legally responsible for that decision. They must know, therefore, what is going on within the charity at all times, and have workable procedures for dealing with emergencies.

Many charities employ staff to carry out the day-to-day management of the charity and employ specialist managers to take care of property or investments, so that it is vitally important that staff and managers in this position should have clear policy guidelines to work to and ready access to the trustees should the need arise.

Contracts with third parties

Contracts made with third parties on the charity's behalf are the legal responsibility of the contracting parties. Where the charity or the trustee body is an incorporated body, such as a limited liability company, the body itself, as a legal person in its own right, is the contracting party and individual members of the body will not, generally, be personally liable. (There is an exception where a company is operating whilst technically insolvent.) Where, however, the charity and the trustees are unincorporated, the trustees themselves will be the contracting parties and if the charity is not able to meet its commitment the trustees will normally be personally liable. Contracting as a charity trustee does not, itself, limit a trustee's potential liability. This underlines the need for trustees to take care never to enter into any commitment on the charity's behalf which the charity's resources will not meet, unless the trustees are prepared to underwrite it personally.

Other situations and activities, such as ownership of property, operations on land or buildings, the employment of staff or fundraising events can also give rise to legal liabilities or other costs. It is wise, in order to protect both the charity and the individual trustees, to insure fully against all usual risks.

Other duties

Charity law imposes a number of more specific duties on charity trustees, for example the requirement to keep accounts and to produce an annual report, to supply certain information and documents to the Charity Commissioners, and to seek the Commissioners' consent to certain transactions. These specific duties are dealt with in detail elsewhere in this book.

Finally, it is worth while for every trustee to bear in mind that the charity has a reputation of its own, which is dependent on the trustees and their staff. A charity may be a landlord, an employer, a neighbour or a provider of services. Trust law does not permit a charity to operate otherwise than in furtherance of its purposes, but there is nothing to prevent it from acting efficiently, fairly and reasonably in its relations with the rest of the world while doing so.

Charitable status – examples

These are some contrasting examples of decisions by the courts and the Charity Commissioners on charitable status which illustrate the fine distinctions which sometimes have to be drawn in interpreting the law.

1 Relief of poverty

A gift for paying for holidays for low-paid employees of a particular firm was held to be charitable, even though the beneficiaries were not a section of the public (1914).

A fund set up by a merchant bank to assist sick or convalescent employees was rejected by the Charity Commissioners since the beneficiaries were not a section of the public and were not in financial need (circa 1980).

2 Advancement of education

A trust under the will of Mrs Bernard Shaw for teaching the Irish the arts of conversation and self-control was held to be charitable as it was educational (1952).

A trust under the will of Mr Bernard Shaw to construct a phonetic alphabet was held to be non-charitable because, although this would have increased knowledge, the will did not provide for the results to be communicated to the public and, in any case, the trust was considered to be political (1957).

3 Advancement of religion

A gift by will to a Carmelite (ie enclosed) order of Nuns was held to be non-charitable because, although this promoted a religious purpose, there could be no proven benefit to the public from private prayer (1949).

A gift to a synagogue which was open only to members was held to be charitable because the worshippers would go out into the community during the rest of the week and, thereby, spread the benefits of religious activity to the public (1966).

4 Other purposes beneficial to the community

A trust under the will of Mr Strakosch to improve relations between English- and Dutch-speaking South Africans was held to be non-charitable because it was considered to be political (1952).

A body established in Birmingham for the promotion of racial harmony within the local community was accepted as charitable by the Charity Commissioners (1982).

Chapter 2
CONSTITUTIONAL REQUIREMENTS

Setting up

Forming a charity is comparable to the procreation of a child. First there is the general idea, then a decision and a series of meetings between the promoters, then a period of gestation and, finally, the day on which the new charity comes into formal existence. Usually, registration follows soon afterwards. Anything may go wrong at any stage until the formal establishment of the charity and, of course, in some instances the infant may be still-born or, if not given proper care and nourishment, it may not survive to maturity.

Some of the excitement and emotional satisfaction associated with the birth of a child are also to be experienced in setting up a new charity. Equally, it has to be said, there are numerous pitfalls and the possibility that the promoters will disagree on the proper direction and development of the infant. In extreme cases there may be abandonment, negligence or an amicable parting of the ways. Unlike a parent, however, the promoter of a charity cannot be made financially liable for its future maintenance, although, if it does not survive he or she, if a trustee, may be required to see that it is duly interred.

The first task in establishing a charity is to determine its purposes, activities, the people who will be involved and the resources which will be available to it. This process, which may take some time, should enable a decision to be taken on the form which the charity will take. Where the charity is to be founded by an individual, a group of people or an existing organisation prepared to donate money at the outset, the classic form of declaration of trust will probably be the simplest and most convenient form of establishing the charity, since it allows considerable control to the founder (or founders). Where, however, a lot of fundraising activity is necessary and a larger number of people will be involved, it may not be practicable to proceed without building in a measure of 'democracy'. In that case, an unincorporated charitable association will be the most appropriate and flexible form of creation. If the charity is to undertake activities involving the employment of a substantial number of staff, or if it will necessarily encounter commercial risks in carrying out its work, a company limited by guarantee may be the best solution. Examples of these three forms of establishing a charity can be found in Appendix A.

Some charities are established by will and it cannot be emphasised too strongly that, if this course is chosen, professional advice should be obtained before the will is made.

There are some other cases. Where the charity is to be a housing association, the best recognised legal form of creation is an industrial and provident society. Where the charity is fortunate enough to have substantial patronage, a Royal Charter may be sought. Occasionally, a charity will be set up by an Act of Parliament.

A certain amount of help can be obtained from the Charity Commissioners and other specialist organisations (some of which are listed in Appendices B and C), but it is generally advisable to seek independent professional advice before finalising the form of a new charity, and essential to do so if there is anything unusual in the proposals.

Choosing the legal form

It should be clear from the outset what the effect will be of choosing one form of establishing a charity over another. Once the charity has been set up the trustees and officers will be bound to observe its terms and follow the procedures which it lays down.

The simplest form to set up and operate is the *declaration of trust*. The trust is not a separate person from its trustees and there are no special formalities apart from: (1) the necessity to have the original document stamped by the Inland Revenue Stamp Office; and (2) the requirements of charity law, including registration in most cases.

An *unincorporated charitable association* is also simple to operate, provided that the terms of the constitution are clear and workable. Again, no separate legal person is created and in this case there is no requirement for a Stamp.

A *charitable company* is a more complex body to operate and should not be undertaken lightly. First, the formalities on setting up the company necessitate registration as a company. It will, therefore, be desirable to use the services of a solicitor, accountant or company formation agent. The company is a separate legal person from those who run it. There are also a number of requirements under company law which will have to be observed in addition to the requirements of charity law. The company must have a registered office (an official address) in England or Wales; it must have a company secretary; annual returns must be submitted to Companies House; accounts must be audited by a registered company auditor (however small the operations may be); a register of members must be kept and an annual general meeting of the members held. There is an important requirement *not* to continue to operate if the company is insolvent, ie if its assets are not sufficient to enable its debts and other liabilities to be met. Company law is underpinned by statutory offences.

Registration

Most charities must be registered with the Charity Commissioners. The main exceptions are 'exempt charities' (see below), charities which do not have land or permanent capital or an income of at least £1000, places of worship registered under the Places of Worship Registration Act 1855 and 'excepted charities', such as voluntary schools.

Exempt charities

Exempt charities consist of certain major charities and types of charities listed in the Second Schedule to the Charities Act 1993. Apart from institutions such as the British Museum, English Heritage and the colleges of Eton and Winchester, they include universities, colleges, grant-maintained schools and charitable societies formed under the Industrial and Provident Societies Acts and charitable Friendly Societies. Exempt charities cannot register, are free from the supervision of the Charity Commissioners and are not subject to the new requirements on charity accounting. Instead, they are subject to other forms of supervision, such as the Universities Funding Council, which generally prescribe their own forms of accounting rules.

Excepted charities

Charities which do not need to register because they are 'excepted' from that requirement, for example voluntary schools, are subject to the Charity Commissioners' supervision and may be required to produce full accounts. The reason why they do not need to be registered is simply that there is a statutory record of their existence elsewhere.

Green form

If a charity will (or may) need to be registered it is sensible (and recognised as good practice) to consult the Charity Commissioners before the draft governing instrument has been finalised. (It is, of course, not usually practicable to do this where the charity is established by will and its terms have already been settled and have come into legal effect by the time the trustees are aware of those terms.) The Commissioners publish a green form containing numerous questions which are designed to assist them in deciding whether or not to accept a proposed (or existing) charity for registration. The Commissioners ask the promoters of new charities (and the trustees of charities which have come into existence but have not been registered) to submit the completed questionnaire with two copies of the (draft) governing instrument, together with any other relevant materials, such as financial records. Considerable care should be exercised in completing the questionnaire, since the questions are not always fully understood on a first reading and an inaccurate response can lead to misunderstanding and serious delay. In some cases it is wise to seek an interview at the Commissioners' office to explain exactly what is proposed.

Name of charity

The Commissioners will also consider the name of the new charity. If they find that it is the same as, or similar to, the name of an existing charity, they may require it to be changed. They may also require a new name to be chosen if the proposed name is misleading or offensive (see Appendix F).

Inland Revenue

Unless the proposals are entirely straightforward and the governing instrument follows one of the recognised model forms, the Commissioners will normally consult the Inland Revenue (Claims Branch) before indicating whether they will accept the proposed charity for registration. This is because the Inland Revenue is a 'person interested' in the registration of a charity, in view of the tax consequences of charitable status. In many cases the Commissioners' approval will be subject to specific alterations being made to the draft governing instrument. Very often, such suggested alterations are based on recognised forms of wording and will assist the Commissioners in advising the charity in future. The alterations should not be adopted, however, unless the proposed charity trustees understand and are entirely happy with them.

Registration number

Once the Commissioners have accepted a proposed charity for registration the trustees may proceed to complete their documents, set up the charity and send in the application form with a certified copy (not the original) of the governing instrument. An Inland Revenue Stamp will be necessary in the case of a declaration of trust. A registration number will then be allocated to the charity, which should be recorded since it will need to be quoted in future correspondence with both the Commissioners and the Inland Revenue.

In addition, many charities like to quote the registration number on their fundraising literature and other documents. A copy of the governing instrument should be given to every trustee and senior officer of the charity and the original should be kept in a safe place, such as a bank.

Significance of registration

The significance of registration is that it provides conclusive proof that the charity is legally a charity and has complied with the legal obligation to register. This does not mean that it is, necessarily, well run. If a charity is, for any reason, not registered, the fact that it is not does not signify that it is not a charity, since charitable status depends on the purposes of the organisation rather than any specific formality. A charity which should be registered, but by some oversight has not been registered, can be registered late, but the trustees may be asked to send the Commissioners more information, including accounts, than is required for a proposed charity.

Anyone may apply to the Commissioners for a copy of the governing instrument, statements of account and other details concerning a registered charity. The basic information is kept on computer and indicates whether the charity concerned has complied with its statutory obligations. Registration underlines the fact that a charity is a public trust, for which the charity trustees are accountable.

Every registered charity with a gross income (ie receipts) of £5000 or more in its last financial year must state the fact that it is registered on all its official documents, including cheques and invoices.

Changing the constitution

Practical experience in administering a charity, or changes in its resources, in the relevant law or in the circumstances of the beneficiaries, or more general changes in society, may convince the trustees that the governing instrument needs to be altered or updated. In extreme cases the purpose of the charity may no longer provide a sensible use for its assets. It is one of the principles of charity law that, if necessary, and provided that the correct procedure is carried out, the purposes or other provisions of a charity's governing instrument may be altered. In fact, it is the trustees' legal duty to take steps to introduce change, where this is necessary in order to make effective use of the charity's resources.

If it appears that an alteration is needed, it is often wise to double check that an unduly restrictive interpretation of the existing document has not been adopted. Sometimes, trustees will be advised that there already exists an implied power to use the charity's resources for the new activity which they have in mind.

If a more liberal interpretation will not assist, or would strain the language of the governing instrument, the next question is whether there is a specific power to alter the instrument.

Alteration to memorandum and articles of association

There is a power to alter the memorandum and articles of association of a charitable company, but if a change to any part of the memorandum (or to any provision in the articles which governs the use of the charity's assets) is envisaged, the Charity Commissioners' consent will be needed in advance and it will be necessary to follow the procedures of company law to effect the required change. Failure to lodge the Commissioners' consent constitutes an offence under company law.

The Commissioners are unlikely to give their consent without good reason and will normally expect the new purposes to be akin to the original purposes. A fundamental change, for example to assist old people instead of children or vice versa, or to benefit the inhabitants of a completely different geographical area, is not likely to be accepted by the Commissioners, without at least negotiating some special arrangement to keep any existing assets available for the old purposes.

Express power of alteration

There is often an express power of alteration in the constitution of an unincorporated charitable association. If such a power exists the procedures must be followed meticulously. This, generally, means notifying the members in advance and calling a general meeting. If a change in the purposes is envisaged, it is wise to consult the Charity Commissioners well in advance, even where the constitution does not specifically require this. The same applies in the case of a declaration of trust which contains an express power of alteration.

If the governing instrument does not contain a power of alteration, or if the power in question does not extend to the sort of alteration envisaged (eg where it specifically excludes a change in the purposes of the charity) and the trustees are convinced that the purposes should be altered, there are two alternative procedures, depending on the size of the charity.

1 Statutory power
If the annual income of the charity is less than £5000 the trustees have a statutory power to pass a resolution (by a two-thirds majority) to alter the

purposes or administrative provisions. The terms of the resolution must be sent to the Charity Commissioners and a notice of concurrence must be received from them before the change can take place. The trustees should advertise their proposals and seek comments from the public, but the method of doing so is for them to decide. Any new purposes must be akin to the original purposes.

2 Scheme

In other cases, it will be necessary to apply to the Charity Commissioners for a scheme. A scheme is a legal document, equivalent to a court order, which modifies or replaces the existing governing instrument. Many older charities are now governed entirely by a scheme or series of schemes. The Commissioners have considerable experience of making schemes and have developed an extensive body of precedents. The procedure is as follows.

Procedure

The trustees should first write to the Commissioners or seek an interview to explain the difficulties in administering the charity under its present governing instrument and identifying every difficulty. They should be ready with their ideas for a more workable arrangement but be prepared to consider alternatives which the Commissioners, from their experience of similar situations, may suggest. Once the Commissioners are satisfied of the need for a scheme and have agreed on what it is broadly to achieve, they will invite the trustees to make a formal application. Once made, such an application cannot be withdrawn unless the Commissioners agree.

The Commissioners will then prepare a draft scheme for the trustees to consider. When any necessary modifications have been made to the draft the trustees are required to arrange the publication of notices, which may be posted in the area of benefit in the case of a local charity or published in a suitable newspaper or journal, inviting members of the public to put forward objections or suggestions to the Commissioners. If the proposals are controversial the proposed scheme may have to be modified or even abandoned, or the Commissioners may decide that any scheme should be made by the High Court. In view of this, it is prudent for the trustees to identify and deal with potential objections to a scheme before publication of the notices.

Assuming that there are no objections (which is usually the case) or that the objections can be overcome, the Commissioners will seal the new scheme, thus bringing it into effect, once they have received evidence of publication from the trustees.

The remaining step is the publication of final notices to the effect that the

scheme has been established, which sets the time-limit for the rare procedure of appealing against the scheme to the High Court.

The trustees will not need professional advice concerning the establishment of a scheme unless the Commissioners require them to obtain it (for example where the trustees are seeking wider powers of investment) or, in some cases, the trustees have specific proposals of their own and wish to formulate them in detail, rather than simply relying on the Commissioners' recommendations.

Cy près doctrine

A scheme may either alter the administrative arrangements of the charity, for example by changing the composition of the body of trustees, or it may alter the purposes of the charity, or both. Where the purposes are to be altered the Commissioners are bound by the cy près doctrine, a Norman–French expression which goes back to the 14th century and means 'close to' or 'akin to'. The existence of this doctrine is one of the reasons why some charities have survived for hundreds of years and still perform a useful and relevant function. It requires the Commissioners (or the court), when altering the purposes of a charity, to keep as close as reasonably practicable to the original purpose, to respect the spirit of the original gift and, as far as possible, to respect the intention of the founder of the charity. It is, therefore, a protection for, and encouragement to, the founders of charities and those who subsequently make gifts to them. A good cy près scheme will enlarge the discretion of the trustees by not being too specific about the method of fulfilling the charity's purpose, thus enabling the charity to adapt to future changes in the surrounding circumstances.

Reviewing aims and procedures

As a general rule, it is a good idea for trustees to give serious consideration to a charity's purposes, administrative provisions and general direction at least once in every generation and more frequently when the charity is operating in a rapidly changing field. In addition, changes in local government or health service administration or in recommended methods of treatment, or changes in local or central Government provision or grant-making policies, or the establishment of other organisations operating in the same field, can all provide specific reasons to consider change.

The new governing instrument

Once a charity's governing instrument has been altered or replaced the trustees have a duty to supply the Commissioners promptly with a copy of the

new document, unless it is a scheme made by the Commissioners themselves (in which case they will already have a copy). The original of the new document should be kept in a safe place with the earlier documents and a copy should be supplied to each of the trustees and senior officers.

Amalgamation

It may be desirable to amalgamate two or more charities which have compatible purposes, in order to achieve synergy, including economies of scale, and to avoid duplication of effort. There are various practical questions which must be resolved, for example who will be trustees, whether all existing staff will continue to be employed, what the name of the new charity will be and where it will have its headquarters, etc. Serious consideration of these matters must be undertaken and adequate time and discussion should be allowed to find the best available solution.

Transfer of assets

There are several, possible, legal methods of achieving amalgamation, depending on the original governing instruments. The simplest method is for one charity to wind up under a power contained in its constitution and transfer its assets over to another charity, which may, or may not, effect some alteration in its name or governing instrument as a consequence. This may give rise to difficulties, however, if, for example, the charity which has been wound up has been left a legacy or is entitled to payments under covenant.

A more tactful method of achieving amalgamation is to set up a new charity incorporating elements from the original charities, which then wind up and transfer their assets to the new charity. The same problem regarding legacies can, of course, arise, but this may be avoided if the new constitution expressly indicates that it is an amalgamation of the existing charities, and identifies them.

Where this arrangement is not constitutionally possible owing to the absence of a power to wind up (or an absence of a power to make an alteration which can legally enable a power to wind up to be adopted) there are two methods of achieving an amalgamation, depending on the size of the charity.

1 Statutory power
If a charity's income does not exceed £5000 and the charity does not hold land which is used for charitable purposes, the trustees are permitted, by

statute, to pass a resolution (by a two-thirds majority) to transfer the assets
to another charity having similar objects. They may then give public notice
of the proposal, notify the Commissioners, obtain a notice of concurrence
and put the transfer into effect. Once the charity's assets have been transferred
the trustees of the transferring charity should send the final statement of
account to the Commissioners with a request that the charity should be
removed from the register of charities.

2 Scheme

In other cases the appropriate procedure will be to apply to the Commissioners for a scheme, which may either simply authorise the transfer of
assets or, if the situation requires more elaborate arrangements, take the form
of a cy près scheme formally providing for the charities concerned to 'be
administered as one charity'. The cy près procedure enables the original
charities to continue to exist in a technical sense, so that the new, combined
charity is, thus, entitled to any covenanted payments or legacies to which
the original charities are, or may become, entitled.

Winding up

Some charities continue indefinitely; others, such as appeal funds, have a
limited lifespan from the outset and cease to exist once their purposes have
been achieved and their assets have been used. In other cases a charity
may be brought to an end deliberately, either in the course of a de facto
amalgamation, or to replace an existing, unincorporated association with a
charitable company. A charity may also be brought to an end because it has
ceased to be financially viable or to perform a useful function.

A charitable company may be wound up and ought to be wound up (or
at least should cease to operate) if it becomes insolvent, ie if its assets will
not cover its liabilities. The memorandum of association will normally state
that any assets remaining after all liabilities have been met should be transferred to another charity having similar objects or, failing that, should be
applied for some other charitable purpose. It is wise to attempt to find a
recipient charity which is carrying on work which the defunct charity would
have supported if it had been able to do so, and to ensure that the recipient
charity is registered (if it is liable to be registered) and is up to date with its
accounts. If the remaining assets are sufficient, or if the purposes to be
supported are being carried on by different charities, there may be more than
one recipient.

There is no reason why a recipient charity should not be a charity which
is administered by one or more of the charity trustees of the defunct charity,

provided, of course, that the purpose of the recipient charity is similar. That should not, however, be the only reason for choosing that recipient. The trustees retain, to the end, their fiduciary duty to apply the charitable funds conscientiously for the purposes for which they were contributed, and must be prepared to justify their decisions on objective grounds.

Express power to wind up

In the case of a charitable unincorporated association or a modern declaration of trust, it is usual to find an express power to wind up and a direction to apply the remaining assets (if any) in a similar way. If there is no power of dissolution, but there is a power of amendment which is not expressly restricted, it may legally be possible to adopt an amendment to the constitution which confers a power of dissolution. It is advisable to consult the Charity Commissioners or an independent legal adviser before doing so, to ensure that the power is properly exercised and cannot be challenged at a later date.

Once a charity has been dissolved and its remaining assets transferred, the last trustees should write to the Charity Commissioners with a copy of the final statement of account, showing that no assets remain, and ask the Commissioners to remove the charity from the register. The Commissioners are bound to remove any charity which has ceased to exist or to operate.

Statutory power

Where a charity is governed by declaration of trust or by scheme there may be no power of dissolution or amendment. If, particularly in the case of an older trust or a charity governed by a scheme, there is any permanent capital (technically called permanent endowment meaning that the charity has the use of the income but must preserve the capital) there will generally be no power to wind up the charity. However, there is such a power if the charity's gross income in the last financial year was no more than £1000 and none of its permanent endowment consists of land. In the case of a very small, permanently endowed charity in this category there is a statutory power to pass a resolution by a two-thirds majority, enabling the permanent capital to be treated as income (and thus spent), provided that there is no suitable charity to which the assets can instead be transferred, that public notice of the proposal is given and that the Charity Commissioners' notice of concurrence is obtained.

Scheme

In all other cases, if the charity ceases to be viable or effective the only practicable solution is to apply to the Charity Commissioners for a scheme to make some workable provision for the application of the income. In this way, charities which were originally engaged in their own specific activities, such as running a school or a group of almshouses, which eventually became unworkable or uneconomic, may eventually be transformed into grant-making trusts or amalgamated with larger institutions. In this way, they continue to be useful and to contribute to the main purpose which the founder intended.

Powers of Commissioners to wind up

Finally, it must be pointed out that if the trustees of a charity misapply its assets the Commissioners will not remove its charitable status. There are various remedial steps open to them, one of which is to order the transfer of the charity's assets to another charity and the winding up of the abused charity. This may be accompanied by taking proceedings against the trustees for breach of trust.

Cy près schemes – examples

The following examples illustrate schemes which have been made, or on which decisions have been taken, where the original purposes of the charities were no longer viable.

Roman's bequest for games which would have been illegal: memorial to testator in some other way (about 300 AD).

Surplus almshouse land: used for school (18th century).

Trust to maintain bishopric in America: trust to maintain bishopric in Canada (19th century).

Elizabethan charity for the redemption of captives of the Barbary pirates: trust for educational purposes (19th century).

Ancient charities for prisons: trust for relief of poverty (19th century).

Ancient charity for boys out of control: boys' public school (19th century).

Historic almshouse building no longer required for housing purposes: museum (1961).

Charity to relieve the poor rate: trust to benefit inhabitants generally (1971).

Trust to provide 11 barrels of white herrings and eight barrels of red herrings to the poor of a fishing village: trust for relief of need in the area (1973).

Teetotal village hall: alcoholic drinks permitted (1975).

Hospital which closed: trust to relieve the sick (1976).

Appeal fund to provide village hall (never built) to commemorate the Coronation: provision of a public clock and garden to commemorate the Queen's Silver Jubilee (1977).

Ancient charity to give loans to young men: trust for education and advancement in life for young people (1988).

Elizabethan charity to maintain trunk road through London: trust to benefit inhabitants of relevant boroughs (1989).

Old charities to provide grazing rights for freemen of borough and their widows: trust for benefit of all the inhabitants (1993).

Chapter 3
MONEY AND PROPERTY

Accounting

It is clear that anyone who controls public money should keep a careful record of it and be accountable to the public for its use. The accounting requirements of charity trustees, which have recently been revised, are, therefore, rightly emphasised. Whatever other economies are adopted, the area of financial control and accountability should not be skimped, even if this involves expenditure which does not directly further the charity's purposes.

Financial records

The law requires every charity to keep financial records which are capable of disclosing its financial position from day to day. This does not necessarily require the employment of a full-time bookkeeper, but does indicate that all payments and receipts should be recorded on a regular and frequent basis. The records must be preserved and must be available for inspection for at least six years, even if the charity goes out of existence in that time. It is, therefore, essential to set up a foolproof system which ensures that these requirements are complied with.

Except for exempt charities, charitable companies and those too small to register, the trustees of every charity must produce a formal report, once a year, consisting of: (1) a narrative report; (2) a balance sheet; and (3) an income and expenditure account. In the case of registered charities and those which ought to be registered, the annual report and statements of account must be sent to the Commissioners within 10 months from the end of the charity's financial year. Other charities must be prepared to produce these records on request.

If the charity's receipts for the financial year in question do not amount to more than £25,000, the statements of account may take a simplified form, which does not include any sophisticated financial analysis but merely records assets and liabilities and payments in and out. If the charity's receipts are more than £25,000, full accounts must be produced. The contents of the annual report and statements of account are laid down by regulations, which are based on a careful study of best practice by experts in charity finance.

Independent audit
An independent audit or examination of accounts on an annual basis is recognised as one of the best ways of ensuring probity and the accurate

presentation of the trustees' stewardship of the charity's assets. Charitable companies are required by company law to produce annual statements of accounts audited by a registered auditor. Exempt charities are governed by their own rules, for example the requirements of the Housing Corporation. In other cases, unless the charity's governing instrument contains a more stringent requirement or the Charity Commissioners formally request an audit, there is no need for a professional audit for a charity whose income (or expenditure) in the previous financial year (or the year before) was not more than £100,000. Instead, it is sufficient for the accounts to be examined by an 'independent examiner', ie a person whom the trustees reasonably believe to have the necessary knowledge and experience to carry out this task and who is not a trustee, founder or beneficiary of the charity or closely connected with such a person. For smaller charities, it may be suitable to ask a friendly bank manager to carry out the examination. For larger charities, it will be more suitable to appoint a qualified accountant, although he or she need not be a registered auditor. If a charity's income was more than £100,000 in the previous financial year, a professional audit by a registered auditor (ie someone qualified to carry out company audit) is required.

It is wise for the trustees to have an annual meeting with the charity's auditor or independent examiner. This provides an opportunity to discuss any problems relating to financial record-keeping and gives the trustees an insight into the way in which the finances of the charity may be perceived by an outsider. It is not uncommon for the auditor to come up with helpful suggestions about financial control.

If the auditor or independent examiner has reason to suspect fraud or other financial wrongdoing, he or she will be expected to report the finding direct to the Commissioners.

Public rights of inspection

The reports and statements of account must be kept for at least six years. They will also be retained by the Charity Commissioners and made available to anyone who wishes, for any reason, to see them or to take a copy. In addition, there is now a statutory duty on charity trustees to provide, within two months, a copy of the latest statements of account (but not the narrative report) to any member of the public who makes a written request to the charity itself. The charity may charge the enquirer a reasonable fee to cover copying and postage costs. Rather than regarding this as an irksome chore, some charities may find that the interest shown by a member of the public in asking for the accounts provides an additional opportunity for seeking gifts or legacies, or making the charity better known.

Failure to account

Persistent failure without reasonable excuse to comply with any of the accounting requirements is an offence.

Tax and rates

Apart from the Council Tax, which applies to domestic property, and VAT, where, despite constant campaigning by charities, the reliefs are piecemeal and highly specialised, charities and those people who give to charities benefit from generous and long-standing reliefs from tax. Charities also benefit from relief from non-domestic rates. It has been said that the reason for this generosity is that charities were performing public service tasks before taxation (and certainly before income tax) was introduced; taxing charities would, therefore, benefit no one. Be that as it may, the existence of tax reliefs is a strong, motivating factor for those contemplating setting up or supporting a charity and it is open to any individual taxpayer to avoid paying tax by making (larger) charitable contributions instead.

Income and capital gains

No charity should pay tax on its income or capital gains. Relief is available, as of right, on receipts from all sources except trading (other than trading in direct furtherance of the charity's purposes or by beneficiaries of the charity), provided that the receipts are used or applied for charitable purposes or for one of the ancillary purposes (such as 'qualifying expenditure' or a 'qualifying investment') recognised by statute. Trading which does not directly further the charity's purposes (eg the selling of Bibles by a religious charity), is incapable of being a charitable purpose in itself, and an investment or item of expenditure which falls outside the category of 'qualifying' expenditure will rarely occur and scarcely ever be necessary. Where tax, for example corporation tax on company dividends, is deducted at source the charity should promptly claim repayment from the Inland Revenue.

Property used for charitable purposes

A charity in rateable occupation of land and buildings is entitled, as of right, to 80 per cent relief from non-domestic rates on property used wholly or mainly for charitable purposes, or for fundraising. In addition, the local authority has a discretion to grant further relief up to 100 per cent, although this must generally be applied for, and justified, every year.

Payments from supporters

Where a supporter gives a charity a sum of at least £250 (the current lower limit for 'gift aid') or makes a deed of covenant in its favour to pay an annual sum of any amount for at least three years, both supporter and charity benefit. The payment is tax-deductible and the charity is entitled to claim from the Inland Revenue the amount of tax for which the supporter would have been liable if the payment had not been made to the charity. (For a suggested form of deed of covenant, see Appendix A.)

Payroll Deduction Scheme

Under the Payroll Deduction Scheme, an employee whose employer participates in the Scheme is able to make automatic tax-deductible gifts from his or her earnings to an agency charity, which may then reclaim the notional tax.

Gifts

Gifts to charity which would otherwise attract capital gains tax or inheritance tax are exempt, but there is no additional benefit from the Inland Revenue for the charity. This situation arises where a gift of land, chattels or investments is made to a charity by will or during the donor's lifetime.

Inland Revenue guidance

The Inland Revenue (Claims Branch) produces some very helpful guidance, as well as official forms, for use by charities and their supporters. It is recognised generally that gifts to charity should be encouraged and that charities should be encouraged to take advantage of the tax reliefs available to them. Indeed, trustees could be held liable for a breach of trust if they caused the charity an actual or notional loss by failing to take advantage of the available tax reliefs. In complex cases, where the situation is not covered by Inland Revenue forms or guidance, professional advice from a lawyer or accountant will be desirable.

Insurance

Fire, other damage and theft

Charity trustees should insure property belonging to the charity against the usual risks such as fire, other damage and theft. Although the basic rule of trust law is that trustees may insure property up to two-thirds of its value, it has been recognised for many years that in the case of charities, full reinstatement value is appropriate if this is possible. Certain charities whose assets, including major works of art, are irreplaceable, have chosen, as a matter of policy, to protect those assets in some other way, such as stringent security precautions, and not to insure. Whilst security precautions which are consistent with the purposes of the charity are prudent and may, indeed, help to reduce the premium payable, it is, generally, only in the most exceptional cases and after full consideration of all the implications, that a body of charity trustees will escape criticism if it decides not to insure the charity's property. For the great majority of charities, such insurance is essential.

Vandalism and terrorism

Charities with buildings in vulnerable places must now consider insurance against the risk of deliberate damage from vandalism and terrorism.

Public and employer's liability

Insurance is also required against the risk of public liability and employer's liability. Failure to insure against these risks renders the trustees potentially liable on a personal basis, if the charity is unincorporated.

Fidelity insurance

A connected issue is fidelity insurance, where an agent or employee of the charity has, in practice, to be given a large measure of responsibility and cannot be supervised constantly by the trustees.

Particular risks

In some circumstances, it may be desirable to take out specific insurance against a particular risk on an ad hoc or short-term basis. For example, insurance might be needed if the charity had received a legacy which it plans to spend, but there is a chance that a relative or dependant of the deceased can make a successful claim under the Inheritance (Provision for Family and Dependants) Act 1975.

Liability insurance

A relatively new area of insurance, which can provide additional protection for charity trustees in certain cases, is liability insurance. This insurance protects a trustee against the possibility of having to meet, personally, a liability arising from a breach of trust, or breach of duty towards the charity (except a wilful or criminal breach of duty) or under a contract. Trustees may always insure themselves, at their own expense, against such liability, but in some cases there may be justification for the charity to pay the premium. The payment of such a premium amounts to a benefit to the trustee who is covered and, therefore, is not permitted, unless it is authorised by the Charity Commissioners (or the court) or specifically provided for in the charity's constitution. The kind of situation in which the Commissioners are likely to be sympathetic to a proposed change in a charity's governing instrument in order to permit such a payment, or an application for a special order to authorise it, is where there is some exceptionally serious risk of liability or where the liability itself could be very great, and it can be demonstrated that it may be difficult to find trustees if the cover cannot be provided at the charity's expense.

Other means of financial protection

In cases where insurance cannot be obtained by the charity there are other methods of obtaining financial protection. In some cases, a person or body other than the charity will have an insurable interest in the subject matter, for example where a painting or sculpture is lent by a charity to a museum or gallery, which itself undertakes to insure it. In other cases, for example where the risk in question is a commercial risk, it may be necessary to consider setting up a limited liability company, which may not itself be a charity, to carry out the activity which gives rise to the risk. This arrangement is common where a charity wishes to raise money through some trading activity (see 'Trading' at p 42 below).

Investment

Charity money which is not due to be spent in the near future should be working for the charity. Funds which will be required within a short time should be placed on deposit at a recognised bank or building society, or some other short-term arrangement should be made to preserve it safely.

Where it is known that funds will not be required for some time, and it is possible to calculate the amount which will then be needed, it is worth considering investment in a short-dated Government Stock or some other short-term investment. It is sometimes possible to achieve capital growth in this way by careful planning and timing.

In the case of permanent endowment or capital funds which are unlikely to be required for several years ahead, the trustees are able to take a longer view and consider specifically not only the charity's need for income but also the desirability of achieving capital growth. Generally, growth is most likely to be obtained by investing in unit trusts, shares in companies or land and buildings, and by being in a position to leave the funds in an invested state until the time for disposing of the investments is ripe.

Common investment funds

A sensible choice for many bodies of trustees is to invest in a common investment fund ('CIF'), which is itself a charity and is established exclusively for the investment of charity funds. A CIF operates in a similar way to a unit trust but is able to pay its dividends gross. Common deposit funds ('CDFs') are similarly available to charities. The best known of the CIFs are the Charities Official Investment Fund and the National Association of Almshouses Common Investment Fund, but several new CIFs have been set up in recent years.

A charity may always invest in a CIF, whatever its powers of investment, and may always invest in narrower range investments under the Trustee Investments Act 1961 (ie Government stocks and certain other traditional investments, such as National Savings Bonds). The extent to which a charity has power to invest outside these areas depends on whether its governing instrument contains an express power of investment.

Powers of investment

Modern governing instruments nearly always contain unrestricted investment powers, enabling the trustees to choose any form of investment, whether in the UK or abroad. Normally, however, trustees should avoid the acquisition of property which does not produce any income or which is in any way speculative, including an unsecured loan, since such a choice is not compatible with the trustees' role of obtaining income to use for the charity's purposes, while protecting the charity's assets. Investment abroad can produce practical difficulties, for example in undertaking transactions from a distance and keeping a close watch on the relevant market. Traded options and unquoted investments can be dangerous unless expert advice is obtained. Some more traditional forms of investment can also be imprudent, for example the purchase of undated stocks, loans on the mortgage of property, partly paid shares, or deferred or non-voting shares.

Statutory powers
Where there is no express power of investment in the governing instrument the trustees are limited to the statutory powers contained in the Trustee

Investments Act 1961, which may, at some stage, be amplified, in the case of charities, under recent legislation. The Act enables trust funds to be invested in a range of UK company securities and authorised unit trusts ('the wider range') only if a division of the fund is first made. One half of the fund must then be kept in the narrower range, whereas the other half may be invested in either narrower- or wider-range investments. Each part of the fund will then grow at its own rate, with accretions (such as bonus issues) being added to the part of the fund from which they are derived.

Schemes
The Charity Commissioners are prepared, in the case of substantial charities having invested funds of £1m or more, to make schemes, widening or updating the investment powers so as to confer a greater discretion on the trustees. This kind of scheme will not, generally, be available unless the trustees have a reasonable track record of investment success and can produce professional advice to the effect that the charity would benefit from wider powers.

Advice on investments

The Trustee Investments Act 1961 requires trustees to obtain advice on all investment decisions, except for investment in Part I of the narrower-range (the simplest and most traditional forms of investment). Trustees should bear in mind the desirability of spreading their funds between a number of investments, rather than keeping all their eggs in one basket. It is essential that the trustees should obtain advice from a stockbroker, merchant banker or other reputable financial adviser who has substantial experience and is either registered or exempt from registration under the Financial Services Act 1986. It is desirable to obtain such advice and to instruct the adviser to keep the charity's investments under review, even where the trustees themselves include someone with relevant experience.

Investment advisers
In some cases, particularly larger charities, the trustees will not be in a position personally to manage the charity's investment portfolio. It may, therefore, be wise to appoint either an investment adviser or some other expert to undertake this task and delegate the power to acquire and dispose of investments to that person or firm. Charity law is not altogether clear on this point, and the official view until recently used to be that so long as the trustees themselves have regular meetings with the expert, set the investment policy under a written agreement, confine the expert strictly to the charity's legal powers of investment, receive prompt and regular reports of all transactions, reserve the power to cancel the arrangement at any time, and review

it every two years, the trustees are unlikely to be criticised for delegating the investment management in this way. On the other hand, they will in that case be regarded as responsible in law for all the decisions made and actions taken by the expert. A safer approach, to which the Charity Commissioners now subscribe, is that the trustees should adopt an express power of delegation either by alteration to the charity's constitution or by applying to the Commissioners for a scheme or order to authorise the delegation.

Holding of investments

The normal rule is that the investments should be held in the name of the charity or the trustee body, if incorporated, or in the names of the individual trustees. Before September 1992, charity investments could be held in the name of the Official Custodian for Charities; a highly convenient system which was free of charge. Recent legislation has abolished the Official Custodian's function of holding investments for charities, except in cases where the Commissioners direct that the Official Custodian will hold them for the protection of the charity's assets. As a result, those investments already held by the Official Custodian are gradually being divested and returned to the trustees. For some trustees, this may be the first time that they have held investments on behalf of a charity (or at all).

It is not, of course, convenient for the investments to be held by a number of individual trustees in the long term, since trustees change and records, therefore, have to be updated in order to avoid difficulties later. Accordingly, it is permissible for the trustees to appoint a nominee, who may either be an individual (eg an ex officio trustee) or a corporate body (eg a nominee company) to hold the investments which were formerly held by the Official Custodian on behalf of the trustees and subject in every way to their control.

Other arrangements are possible. Where there is scope for a two-tier governing body, it is often convenient to appoint a trust corporation or other more or less permanent body to hold the investments safely for the charity whilst the day to day investment and other management decisions are taken by the more rapidly changing body of charity trustees. Where this system has been set up formally, the holding body, if it is a trust corporation, may be designated the custodian trustee and the charity trustees designated the managing trustees.

Incorporation

A two-tier structure is not always desirable, particularly if there is likely to be a good deal of movement in the funds. In such cases, if the charity is not itself incorporated it may be wise to consider incorporation of the trustee body under the Charities Act 1993. By this procedure, which involves an application to the Charity Commissioners for a certificate of incorporation, the trustee body is given a name and legal personality of its own. This can bring considerable administrative benefits, not least in the holding of investments, as well as incidentally protecting the trustees from direct personal liability towards outside parties. An alternative would be to set up a limited liability company and seek an order of the Commissioners for its appointment as trustee of the charity, the effect of such order being to constitute the company as a trust corporation for the purposes of that charity only.

Land investment

Some charities have power to invest in land, which may be an express power or a power implied from the fact that the charity already holds land as an investment. The Commissioners may also make an ad hoc order authorising a charity to purchase land as an investment, if the Commissioners are provided with evidence, in the shape of a report from a qualified surveyor, which demonstrates that the proposed investment is in the charity's interests. (See further 'Land and buildings' below.)

Land and buildings

Buildings (except caravans and other removable structures) legally form part of the land on which they are built. Therefore, for convenience, wherever 'land' is referred to in this book any buildings on the land are included in that expression.

Charities own land for two main purposes: as an income-producing investment or for their own use. It is worth noting that, judging by past history, land has performed as a better, long-term investment for charities than any other investment. The endowments of very old, established charities which are well-endowed today all consisted of land, some of which was of very little value at the outset. Functional land includes almshouses, village halls, recreation grounds, art galleries, museums, places of worship, church halls, schools, hospitals, hostels, swimming pools, historic monuments, archaeological sites, community centres, leisure centres, libraries, women's refuges and the administrative offices of charities.

Land may be held freehold or leasehold or may be rented or hired. Where the charity owns a freehold or leasehold interest the trustees are subject to a number of responsibilities as property-owners. They are obliged to make arrangements for repairs and insurance to the extent that these duties are not undertaken by anyone else. In addition, where they occupy land they are liable for non-domestic rates and water rates.

In the case of leasehold land, charities will be responsible for paying the rent and observing the covenants in the lease.

Holding of land

Title to land is normally held in the name of the charity or the trustee body, if incorporated, or in the name of a custodian trustee, or in the names of the individual trustees, where neither the charity nor the trustee body is incorporated and there is no custodian or corporate holding trustee.

If individual trustees hold the land there is no upper limit on their number (as there would be with a private trust), but there must be at least two individual trustees in order to give a valid receipt for capital money, ie to be able to sell, mortgage or exchange the land or grant a lease at a premium. This immediately gives rise to the problem that unless every new trustee is appointed by deed and amendments are made to the particulars kept at the Land Registry (if the land is registered), the title will be vested in a dwindling number of individuals, some of whom may cease to be trustees, and technical problems may arise when it is necessary, at some future date, to prove the charity's ownership.

This problem can be overcome by one of two methods.

1 Certificate of incorporation

When the land is held on a short lease, or it is expected that there will be frequent transactions, as where land is held as an investment and leases will need to be granted or enforced from time to time, or where the land is likely to be sold, it is appropriate to consider applying to the Charity Commissioners for a certificate of incorporation under the Charities Act 1993 (see 'Incorporation' at p 29 above). Alternatively, and less simply, it may be considered wise to set up a limited liability company to be appointed as the trustee, or holding trustee, of the charity.

2 Land vested in the Official Custodian

In cases where the land is likely to be held for many years to come, for example where it constitutes a permanent endowment of the charity and is used for its charitable purposes, the ideal solution is to apply to the Commissioners for an order vesting title to the land in the Official Custodian for Charities. In some cases, assistance from the charity's legal adviser may be necessary. The Official Custodian then, technically, holds the title and in the case of registered land is recorded as the proprietor at the Land Registry, but has no personal responsibilities and powers of management. All powers and responsibilities remain with the charity trustees, who are entitled to enter into agreements or take proceedings relating to the land in the name of the Official Custodian.

Sale, exchange or leasing of land

Until 31 December 1992, charities were frequently required to obtain the Charity Commissioners' consent, or an order excepting the charity from the requirement to obtain consent, to the sale, exchange or leasing of land. A new system has now been introduced whereby, in most cases, the transaction can go ahead without any involvement by the Commissioners.

Exempt charities have never had to obtain the Commissioners' consent, but may be required to obtain the consent of some other body, for example the Housing Corporation in the case of a registered housing association.

Consent is not required where the charity disposes of land to another charity, or leases it to a beneficiary, in accordance with the express provisions in the trusts. There is also no need for consent where the transaction is authorised by an Act of Parliament or a scheme made by the Commissioners (or the court).

In all other cases, consent is always required where the other party to the transaction is one of the trustees or a donor to the charity, or a person closely connected by a family or business relationship with a trustee or donor, where the charity will not get the best price or rent obtainable, or where the procedures laid down in the legislation cannot, for some reason, be carried out. In those cases, consent must be obtained *before* the trustees commit themselves to the deal and the Commissioners, who will need to be satisfied that the transaction is in the charity's interests, will inform the trustees of their detailed requirements.

New procedure
In the majority of cases the trustees will have to follow the new procedure, which is designed to safeguard both the charity and the trustees personally. Before committing themselves to any transaction, (ie in the case of a sale, before exchanging contracts) the trustees must instruct an independent, qualified surveyor (who may be the estate agent who finds the purchaser for the charity but not the agent who approaches the charity on behalf of a prospective purchaser) to make a written report on the proposed transaction, which covers all the items listed in the regulations including the measurements of the land, any planning permission, and the value of the land, and to advise on the best method of marketing and disposing of the land. The trustees must then carry out any marketing recommended by the surveyor, for example by placing notices at the site or in the local newspaper and reach a positive decision that the proposed terms are the best that the charity can obtain. Only then may the trustees commit themselves to the transaction.

In the case of functional land, which is held on a formal trust for use for charitable purposes, a sale, exchange or long lease should not take place unless the trusts contain a power of sale (or leasing), since this is inconsistent

with a straightforward trust to use the land for a specified purpose. If there is no power of sale the Commissioners may be willing to make a scheme to confer one. If there is a power of sale and the purpose of the sale is not simply to buy a replacement property, additional steps must be carried out before the land is sold. Whatever marketing arrangements are made the trustees must advertise the proposed sale and invite comments from the public. They must then consider any objections or suggestions received from the public before proceeding.

Simpler arrangements are permitted for short leases without a premium. A lease for up to seven years may be granted without a written report from a surveyor and the surveyor need not be formally qualified as long as the trustees are satisfied that he or she has the necessary knowledge and experience and the terms are the best that can be obtained for the charity. A lease for up to two years, of land held on trust for functional purposes, need not be specially advertised.

Formalities
Specific formalities must be followed in the actual contract, agreement, lease, conveyance, deed of gift or transfer, whenever land is acquired or disposed of by a charity, including an exempt charity. These are designed to make it clear whether the land is subject to the restrictions imposed by law and, in the case of dispositions, whether the procedures have been followed. This is not, therefore, an area of conveyancing which the lay person can expect to be able to undertake without legal advice.

Mortgage of land

Apart from being an investment or a charitable facility, charity land can be a valuable financial resource in the sense that it can be mortgaged in order to secure a loan (for example to fund a project). The new legislation lays down a new procedure for borrowing on the security of charity land without the need for the Commissioners' consent. This involves obtaining advice from a financial expert (who must be entirely unconnected with the lender but may be an employee of the charity) concerning the charity's need to borrow, whether the rate of interest is reasonable and whether the charity can afford the loan charges.

Making grants

Some charities operate entirely by giving grants of money or other forms of financial assistance to individuals or to other charities for furtherance of the charitable purposes of those charities. Some of the smallest and some of the largest charities in the UK operate in this way. Others make occasional grants or loans. If charity money is to be used effectively, sensible methods of selecting recipients, fixing the level and period of support, and following up the way in which the grant has been used should be adopted.

Objective of assistance

First, consideration must be given to the objective of the assistance which is to be given. This will depend on the purpose of the charity, which may be very specific, for example relieving need in a particular area, or very general, eg furthering any charitable purpose at the discretion of the trustees. The purpose of the charity sets the limits for grant-making but, in most cases, since funds are never unlimited, the trustees must take a policy decision on the kinds of grant they will normally consider. Policy decisions are not fixed, and policy decisions are often modified from time to time in the light of experience, the needs of potential recipients and the resources available.

Applications for assistance

Secondly, the trustees must decide whether they will invite applications or find other ways of identifying recipients. This depends largely on the breadth of the purpose and area of benefit and on how close the charity, or its trustees are to the beneficiaries. In the case of a local charity, it may be preferable for the trustees or their staff to find individual beneficiaries through local schools, churches or other organisations, or the local authority, rather than to seek applications. This is important particularly where there may be some doubt about whether those most in need of help will come forward by them- selves. In a large area, and where grants are normally given to charities rather than individuals, postal applications are usual. In those cases, care is needed in targeting potentially successful applicants and designing the application form (if any) to enable the applications to be considered efficiently.

Policy guidelines

When a charity has numerous applications to consider the policy guidelines assist in reducing the number to manageable proportions and it may be sensible to divide the task of giving detailed consideration and carrying out any further investigations between different members of the trustee body. It is the trustees as a whole, however, who are responsible for the allocation of funds.

It is always wise to check on the other sources of funds available to an applicant, the effect (if any) which the proposed assistance will have, in the case of individuals, on any statutory benefits to which he or she is entitled and, in the case of grants to charities, whether they have complied with their obligations to register and submit accounts. It is also prudent to find out exactly what the money will be used for and, in cases of grants to charities, to check that the proposals are within their own objects. These precautions help to ensure that the grant will be effective.

Not every recipient will be well enough organised to manage the grant if it is paid in one lump sum and, in any case, the grant-making charity may not have the whole amount available at once. In such cases the payments may be made by instalments and the grant-making charity may wish to impose conditions, such as receiving an account or a school report and checking that the grant is being used effectively before paying out future instalments. It is not uncommon for grants to be paid over three years or longer.

Monitoring of the use made of grants, by means of spot checks, questionnaires and follow-up correspondence, is generally worth while, since it enables the trustees to keep a check on the effectiveness of the grant and modify their policy and procedures for the future. Provided that the amount is not excessive, the additional time and money will be well spent.

Effectiveness is not everything, however. Unlike statutory bodies spending taxpayers' money under bureaucratic controls, charities are in the fortunate position of being speedy, imaginative and able to conduct small-scale experiments from time to time. They do not exist to ape the provision made by central or local government, but have their own agenda in which they can give help or take initiatives which the statutory system cannot attempt. Independence is a boon, which should be valued. Charities can be originators, experts and leaders in their own fields.

A suggested form of grant agreement between one charity and another appears at Appendix A, Form 5.

Raising funds

Most new charities are not endowed by their founders but must raise funds in order to survive and grow. Some charities need to raise funds for particular projects from time to time. Fortunately, people are generous when they are convinced that their gifts will be put to good use and often even when they are merely attracted by enthusiastic, heart-warming or heart-touching advertisements.

Fundraising is not in itself a charitable purpose, so an organisation set up purely to raise funds is not a charity. However, moderate fundraising, including expenditure for that purpose, is allowable as part of the administration of a charity. If fundraising is likely to involve a substantial amount of cost and effort, and certainly where it will dominate the activities of the charity, it is wise to set up a separate organisation to carry it out (see 'Trading' at p 42 below).

Managing fundraising

Managing the raising of funds has its own expertise, and trustees should not assume that they can be successful fundraisers without taking advice from someone who knows about the problems involved. On the other hand, trustees should be wary of committing themselves to a commercial fundraiser without checking his or her credentials. So many charities have had disastrous experiences with cynical or incompetent 'professionals' that a new law has been introduced to regulate the sort of agreement which is allowed and require disclosure of fundraisers' remuneration. A charity (or its trustees) cannot be held to an agreement which does not comply with the law. It is hoped that the new régime will increase public confidence as well as the confidence of the charities themselves.

Methods of fundraising

There are as many ways of raising funds as human ingenuity can devise and, as with so many other activities, there are fashions which change from time to time. Generally, it is easier to raise money for a cause which appeals to the emotions of prospective donors, and for a specific project rather than for basic running costs. Additional incentives may be provided if the beneficiaries and/or donors are involved in some specific activity, which can be entertaining or instructive in itself, or by the provision of prizes or rewards. Occasionally, two or more charities may combine their efforts in a creative way which helps to put their work into a different perspective.

Restrictions on fundraising

The law impinges on particular types of fundraising activities in different ways.

(1) The regular buying and selling of goods or services is trading and, unless it is carried out in actually furthering the objects of the charity or by the beneficiaries (see under 'Tax and rates' at p 23 above) it will be taxable. Small scale, one-off or occasional trading, such as a jumble sale, a Scouts' Job week or an annual sale of Christmas cards is acceptable, however.

(2) If a professional fundraiser or commercial organisation solicits funds for a charity by means of a broadcast or over the telephone, it is obligatory to provide an opportunity for someone who contributes £50 or more (in the case of a broadcast only if by credit or debit card) to cancel the payment within seven days, and, where goods have been purchased, when they have been returned.

(3) Lotteries are illegal unless the charity is registered with the Gaming Board and the lottery is conducted within the prescribed limits as a Society Lottery.

(4) Advertising and broadcasting is subject to the law of libel and the advertising and broadcasting Codes of Practice, which reflect public opinion on what is fair and decent. As with all advertising, exaggerated claims tend to be counter-productive.

(5) It is wise for charities to beware of political controversy; although views may be strongly held within the organisation itself, it is not the purpose of any charity to campaign for a change in the law, either in the UK or elsewhere. In addition, the expression of seemingly political views usually has negative effects on some potential donors.

(6) Local and road safety regulations may need to be checked where an outdoor activity, such as a bicycle ride, is planned, and permission from land owners affected will be required.

(7) Health and safety regulations, food regulations and licensing laws, as well as the detailed terms of hiring and insuring premises will be relevant where premises are to be used for a sale, a dance or other event which is likely to attract large numbers.

(8) If funds are to be collected from the public by house-to-house collections or in a public place such as the street, a shopping precinct or other place to which the public have access without payment, the charity will need to obtain a permit from the local authority or, if the appeal or flag day is to be nationwide, an order from the Charity Commission. Various conditions are likely to be imposed, including, possibly, conditions to protect public order and traffic control and collectors will be required to have badges and certificates (sometimes combined in one) to prove that they are genuine. The law in this area has recently been overhauled by the Charities Act 1992, Part III.

Fundraising records

It is vitally important to keep careful records of money raised by fundraising efforts and the cost of raising it, both to be able to judge whether a similar effort should be made another time and to report back quickly to supporters on the immediate result, and also to report later on the use to which the funds have been put. It is questionable whether charities are right to suggest to supporters that by giving a stated amount they will enable the charity to do something specific and individual (such as feed a starving child for a month) but it is useful and valuable to be able to point to a particular project or initiative which, through money contributed by the public, has become a reality, and it is arguable that a greater public response will be encouraged if the donors can share the charity's feeling of achievement.

Several of the larger national charities capitalise on this by setting up or encouraging the formation of local or regional 'branches' or groups of 'friends' whose main practical function is to raise funds for the central organisation. It is usual for these groups to be given permission to quote the national charity's registration number while raising funds. This may be sensible and effective in many cases, but it is worth pointing out that the national body must then take responsibility for whatever is said or done in its name. It should also ensure that it has approved the constitution of the local group (and can control any amendments to it) and that it receives the group's accounts, which should be incorporated into its own accounts.

Offences

It is an offence to collect funds from the public without a local authority permit or a Charity Commission order or to fail to comply with the regulations about public collections for charity. It is also an offence to solicit funds for an organisation which is stated to be a registered charity when it is not.

A charity which discovers that an unauthorised person is collecting funds on its behalf is able to apply to the court for an order to prevent it.

Accepting gifts and legacies

It might be supposed that there are no problems for a charity in accepting gifts and legacies. However, it is sometimes necessary to give the matter careful thought.

There may be technical problems connected with gifts and legacies. A gift of anything other than money must be made in the correct manner and in favour of the correct person. There can be serious difficulties in the case of gifts by will if the recipient charity is incorrectly described, and in such cases there may even be competition between charities for the gift.

If it is not clear whether a specific charity is referred to in a will the usual procedure is for the executors to apply to the Treasury Solicitor, who acts for the Attorney-General in his capacity as protector of charities (and would, therefore, be represented in court to protect the interests of charity in general if the matter had to be decided in that way) with a view to ascertaining the Attorney's view of the matter. In many cases the available evidence will give some indication of the charity, or at least the charitable purpose, which the testator intended to support. Provided that the residuary beneficiaries or (if the charity is entitled to the residue) those who would be entitled in the event of a partial intestacy, are content with the proposals, the matter can be dealt with informally and without expense. If necessary, and if everyone with a potential interest is in agreement, the Commissioners will be willing to resolve the problem by making a scheme. A scheme depends on the existence of some kind of trust, however, and if there is no trust there is another procedure, known as the Sign Manual, by which charitable purposes can be attached to a problematic gift. Until the mid-1980s the Sign Manual procedure required the personal signature of the Sovereign, but is now carried out by the Attorney-General in her place.

It is rare for such problems to be referred to the court and, of course, it is desirable that they should not in view of the costs inevitably incurred, which reduce the amount available for charity.

Refusal to accept gift

Occasionally the trustees of a charity, for some good reason, decide that they do not wish the charity to accept a gift. The trustees are not entitled to refuse a gift unless it is impractical or would entail a liability which would outweigh its value. If there is some other reason not to accept it, the trustees should seek the advice of the Commissioners, who may authorise them to decline it. The risk for the trustees if they do not obtain that authority is that, at some later date, they might be required to make good to the charity the amount which their action had caused it to forgo.

Gifts subject to conditions

If the gift is subject to a condition or expressed to be for some particular purpose which does not enable the trustees to pool it with the rest of the charity's resources it may be necessary to register the gift as a 'subsidiary charity' (ie one which is technically a separate charity and which is administered alongside an existing registered charity), and show it separately in the accounts. This happens frequently in the case of school charities, to which former staff and pupils often give a prize fund for particular subjects or sports.

The same principle applies in the case of funds given for a specific purpose during the lifetime of the donor or funds raised by an appeal for a specific project. The money or property which has been given to the charity is held by the trustees on a special trust for that purpose and cannot be treated as part of the charity's general funds.

Failure of purpose

When the funds available cannot reasonably be used for the specified purpose, eg where the cost is too great or planning permission is refused, it is not open to the trustees simply to use the funds for other purposes, unless the terms of the gift or the appeal literature specifically allow for this. In strict law, in these situations the trustees hold the funds on behalf of the donors. If there is a single, identifiable, living donor the problem may quite easily be resolved by going back to him or her, explaining the problem and requesting permission (preferably in writing) to use the funds for another purpose of the charity.

If, on the other hand, it is not possible to identify or trace all the donors, for example where the money has come from cash collections or from a fund-raising concert or other event or where the donor is no longer alive, the purpose can only be altered by a scheme.

There are two procedures associated with the making of a scheme in this situation, depending on whether the gift is made by will or otherwise.

'General charitable intention'

If the gift is made by will the normal procedure, which avoids an application to the court, is first to determine whether there was a 'general charitable intention' on the part of the testator. If so, it is best to reach an agreement between the charity and the residuary beneficiaries or persons who would be entitled on intestacy, obtain the approval of the Treasury Solicitor acting for the Attorney-General on a destination for the fund which is cy près the testator's intention, and then ask the Charity Commissioners to make a scheme to direct the funds for that purpose. The executors will be in charge of the funds and will normally carry out the correspondence until the scheme is made.

Identifiable donors

If the funds have been raised by an appeal, a scheme will not be made until all identifiable donors are contacted and asked either to sign a written disclaimer or ask for their money back. When the scheme has been established the trustees will have to put any funds, given by donors who could not be contacted, aside for six months. This procedure has recently been streamlined and details of the new regulations are available from the Charity Commissioners.

Avoiding failure

In view of the potential difficulties, which can be time-consuming and expensive for the charity, it is prudent to offer advice and guidance to would-be donors, informing them on the purposes for which gifts would be welcome and, above all, making the proper name and address of the charity quite clear to them. Most problems arise where a charity changes its name (or address) or where its publicity material is vague or inaccurate on technical details. In the case of appeals, it is sensible to state an alternative purpose in case the appeal fails to reach or overshoots its target or if the project in question cannot be carried out at the end of the day, and to ask donors to state, when making their contributions, whether they wish to have their money returned in such an event.

Sponsorship

Artists, composers and architects have all relied on the patronage, ie material support and protection, of wealthy and well-placed individuals. From the Enlightenment onwards, charities of all kinds have often had patrons. Today the patronage of a member of the Royal Family, a media star or a representative of excellence in the charity's field of work is regarded by many charities as a valuable asset which can ensure that the charity is taken seriously, adds dignity to formal occasions and helps in fund-raising.

The role of the patron, however, does not now involve the direct provision of cash or commissions. This function has been taken over by the sponsor.

A sponsor is more likely to be a commercial organisation than an individual and is more often limited to a specific project, such as the publication of the charity's newsletter, the provision of equipment to be used by the charity or the support of a particular fundraising event, and is also limited in terms of the amount of support provided. In addition, the sponsor expects to receive a tangible benefit for itself, such as increased public awareness of its goods or services, from its association with the charity.

All kinds of odd combinations, some witty, result from sponsorship agreements by charities, which can be very beneficial to both parties. Care is needed, however, in the initial choice of sponsor, since its own reputation will be linked with the charity's and it could, for example, be embarrassing if an environmental charity was sponsored by an industrial concern which turned out to be a polluter, or a temperance charity to be sponsored by a multi-purpose company which diversified into alcoholic drinks. Charities should also be wary of being so grateful for the sponsorship that they allow the sponsor's name to dominate the charity's publicity. If charitable funds are used to any substantial extent to promote a non-charitable body, the trustees could be liable for a breach of trust and the charity could be taxed on the amount spent.

'Commercial participators'

The Charities Act 1992, Part II, contains new requirements for 'commercial participators' which, like professional fundraisers, are obliged to disclose how much of any promotion, which is stated to be for charity, will actually be given to charity. Commercial sponsors are caught by these provisions and will not be able to get away with the suggestion that all or most of the proceeds of something they sell will be used for charity unless this is strictly true.

Trading

Some charities pursue trading activities in their charitable work. For instance, a charity which runs workshops for disabled people as a method of relieving their disability is carrying out a trade if the goods produced are sold. Similarly, a charity for educational purposes may operate through a fee-paying school or other institution, and it is also common to find the league of friends of a hospital providing extra comforts for the patients by means of a hospital shop or flower stall. However, there are unlikely to be any tax or legal difficulties in these cases.

Trading activities as adjunct to charitable purpose

Where, for example, a university contracts to carry out research for a commercial organisation, a cathedral sells art books or souvenirs or a bar is established in a community centre, the trading activity may enhance, as well as help to finance, the charitable purpose but is an adjunct to, rather than a method of carrying out, the charitable purpose. Caution must be exercised if a trading activity of this kind becomes successful or begins to assume importance as an element in the charity's finances. If the trend continues, it will be necessary to consider hiving off the trading activity to a separate, non-charitable body, usually, but not necessarily, a limited company.

Trading for the purpose of raising funds

Trading which is carried out purely for the purpose of raising funds need have nothing to do with the work or purpose of the charity, although it will often promote its name. For example, the sale of t-shirts and other promotional goods, the issue of gift catalogues, a dining club, a second-hand clothes shop or even a specific business, such as publishing or estate agency, may be conducted exclusively in support of a charity. This does not make the trade a charitable purpose, nor can an organisation devoted to that trade be a charity, even if all the profits are used for wholly charitable purposes. In many cases the trading company will be a 'commercial participator' for the purposes of the Charities Act 1992 (see p 42 above).

It follows that a charity is not in a position to use its funds to support the trading activity since this would normally be an application of funds for a non-charitable purpose and a breach of trust. There are rare exceptions. The purchase of shares in a trading company or the making of a loan at a market rate of interest to a trading body can, in some circumstances, be regarded as a proper investment for the funds of the charity, assuming that its powers of investment are wide enough to permit this and satisfactory financial advice is obtained. In most cases, however, the fact that the charity is asked to provide financial support is an indication of economic weakness on the trading company's part and should sound a clear warning to the trustees that the charity should not allow itself to become too dependent on the trading company or too closely connected with its problems. It is almost always better for the trading body to obtain its finance from an independent source.

When the arrangements are working satisfactorily, they can prove very beneficial. The preferred system is for the trading body, which may be a company or, for example, a social club, to covenant the whole or part of its taxable profits to the charity for a period of at least three years. As a result, the trading body is relieved from tax on the amount paid each year and the charity is entitled to recover the amount in question from the Inland Revenue.

In addition, the charitable relief from non-domestic rates is available for charity shops and commercial outlets within charity premises, and VAT reliefs may be available.

Chapter 4
MANAGEMENT

Choosing trustees

Although the trustees themselves may not consider the personality of the trustees to be important (and the employees of the charity may have a sneaking preference for the kind of trustee who remains in the background), the character of the governing body of a charity is a key to the character and reputation of the charity and may be vital to its success or failure.

People become trustees for a variety of reasons, often subjective, and in a variety of ways, often serendipitous. In some cases, they are elected by the members or appointed by outside bodies, such as the local authority, the parents of the pupils at a school or from the beneficiary class, such as patients suffering from a specific disease or their families or the users of facilities provided by the charity for the community. In such cases, there may be an opportunity for the continuing trustees to influence the appointment or even suggest a particular person. In other cases the trustees are appointed by the continuing trustees directly.

Generally, it is helpful if the trustees have something in common with each other, since this eases communication between them and tends to minimise the scope for sterile arguments about peripheral issues. The most important common interest should, of course, be a sincere desire to carry out the charity's purposes effectively, but successful teamwork can be built up if the trustees also have a specific geographical or religious link, even where the charity is not confined to a particular locality or a particular religious denomination.

There are dangers for the well-being of the charity, however, if the trustees are too closely identified with each other, and especially if two or more of them are related (unless, of course, the charity is a family charity). There are also serious risks of stagnation if the same people remain in office as trustees for years on end, especially where they are all of a similar age.

Ideally, a body of trustees should not be a monoculture but should contain representatives of different occupations, age groups, sexes and social backgrounds, with a regular turnover so that no one becomes indispensable and thus trapped, and new ideas are constantly being brought into the discussions. Arrangements vary, but three years is a reasonable term of office and it is wise to adopt a system under which trustees are required to have a break from their duties after two consecutive terms of office. It should also be possible for trustees to resign when their own circumstances change, without feeling that they are placing an unfair burden on their co-trustees.

The risk of taking on an unknown colleague can be avoided if, in advance of any formal appointment, a prospective trustee is invited to attend a few meetings as an observer. A similar compromise may provide a sympathetic solution to the problem of an elderly trustee, who can no longer be expected to take an active part in the administration of the charity but for whom complete retirement would cause a serious sense of loss.

The qualities which a charity trustee should ideally possess are: genuine concern, rather than cynicism; reliability and judgement, since other people will be affected by the trustees' decisions; a willingness to listen and learn, since in the charity world new developments are taking place constantly; and a measure of toughness in order to safeguard the charity's interests. To the extent that such paragons are not always available, these qualities can be provided in combination by the whole trustee body.

It will also be appropriate to look for specific qualities required by the purposes, organisation and needs of the particular charity. Thus, it is useful to have a medical practitioner on the body of trustees of a charity which promotes medical research or care for the sick; a landowner or property expert where the charity's assets include land and buildings; a mother or teacher where the charity is concerned with young children; and so forth. Any charity can benefit from the contribution of a sympathetic accountant, lawyer or company secretary. Apart from the direct contribution to the trustees' own decision-making, a trustee's expertise can also be useful to the work of any member of the staff of the charity who has the same or a relevant profession or function.

Trustee meetings

The essence of the decision-making process within a charity is the meeting of the trustees. The conduct of meetings may be laid down in detail in the governing instrument, in which case the requirements should be strictly followed but, in addition, charities tend to develop their own traditions, which differ widely. In all cases, the essentials of an effective meeting are adequate preparation, fair and efficient chairmanship and accurate, readable minutes.

Preparation

Before the meeting, the clerk or secretary, or the director of the charity (who in many cases performs the secretarial function at trustee meetings) should discuss with the Chairman the proposed agenda, the order in which items should appear and the timing of the meeting. It is as well to have a proposed time for the end of the meeting as well as the beginning. The notice of the date and time of the meeting, the agenda and any supporting papers should normally be sent to each of the trustees in ample time for them to arrange their diaries and study the papers.

Trustees should be encouraged to give their apologies in advance if they are unable to attend, since this may affect the quorum. In some cases, a meeting may need to be rearranged to suit the timetable of a particular trustee who has some special contribution to make to an item on the agenda. There is no reason why those who cannot attend should not be invited to give their views in advance, but it must always be remembered that they will not have heard the discussion and cannot veto a decision by that means.

Meetings should be held in a quiet environment, with adequate space and where the trustees will not be interrupted.

Quorum

There must be a quorum if the meeting is to take any decisions. Where a meeting is unexpectedly inquorate, it is often worthwhile to continue with the discussion, with a view to ratification of any provisional decisions at the next meeting.

Some trustee bodies do not find it necessary to put a matter to the vote, whilst other bodies vote on every point. Voting should normally be by a show of hands or other tangible indication of preference, given only after full discussion has taken place.

Chairmanship

The chairman's rôle is to conduct the meeting and see that it gets through its business. The purpose of the casting vote is not to give the chairman extra powers but to enable him or her to end the discussion on a particular item. For this reason the convention is that the chairman should not use the casting vote to alter an existing policy or to impose a controversial decision on the trustees. This does not mean that the chairman should be passive. In many cases the chairman exercises leadership which is appreciated by his or her fellow trustees and helps the charity to operate in a dynamic way. On the other hand, the chairman must be fair and try to encourage all the trustees (even recently appointed trustees) to participate.

There will be occasions when it is desirable to invite a person other than the trustees and their secretary to attend a meeting. For example, the meeting may provide a suitable occasion to hear, at first hand, the advice of a professional adviser, or a particular employee may have a report to make or explain. Whatever the trustees' normal habits at meetings, it is worth bearing in mind that the person who has been invited is the trustees' guest for the occasion and should be shown courtesy; he or she should not, for example, be kept waiting and should not be expected to sit through irrelevant agenda items.

Minutes

Minutes should always be taken, since they will constitute the record of what was decided and may have to be referred to at a later date. They may be taken by the secretary, clerk or director or by a trustee or employee chosen for the purpose. They should not be taken by the chairman.

The arrangements should ensure that, within reason, the trustees feel free to speak their minds at the meeting. It is important that the minutes record only what is likely to be useful for the charity's records. Therefore, it is preferable that a person takes the minutes, rather than a mindless tape-recorder, transcription from which would, in any case, be an unpleasant chore.

It is normal practice for the minutes to be circulated in draft to all those who attended the meeting and either approved or corrected at the next meeting, when they should be signed by the chairman. The minutes should then be kept in a safe place and must be available for any trustee to consult.

Frequency of trustee meetings

There should always be at least two meetings of the trustees each year and, in many cases, it will be necessary or desirable to hold considerably more. The precise arrangements will depend on the nature of the charity's work and the extent to which it is carried out by employees, rather than directly by the trustees. There should, in any case, be a procedure for calling a special meeting at short notice to deal with emergencies. There is no excuse for not dealing with a serious problem merely because the next scheduled meeting of the trustees is some months ahead.

In addition, there may be meetings of committees (who must report to the next full meeting if not before) and the occasional social gathering will help to keep the trustees (and others) in touch.

Dealing with professionals

There are numerous occasions in the running of a charity when professional advice is desirable or essential. A charity's needs are different from those of an individual, and trustees, because they are not dealing with their own assets, are more often in the position of requiring professional advice. Obtaining and acting on professional advice can also safeguard the trustees personally from any claim that they have failed in their duties. Trustees should be able to recognise when professional advice should be obtained for the charity and be able, in practice, to obtain it.

Choosing a professional

The correct choice of a professional adviser is vitally important and not always easy. The quality and style of professional people varies considerably and the best recommendation is always one from a similar organisation based on personal experience. In addition to being satisfied of the competence of the adviser and, where appropriate, of professional qualifications and other credentials, trustees must consider two particular factors: fees, and the chemistry of the relationship.

Fees
Professional services cost money and it is a false economy to assume that being a charity will be a passport to free advice of adequate quality. A trustee would not expect to employ, for example, a builder, to work for nothing. Fees are almost always likely to be higher than the trustees think, but they are a proper administrative expense which can and should be budgeted for. It is, therefore, essential to accept that there will be a financial cost and to make sure, at the outset, that the amount involved is known (in broad terms) and that the charity can afford that cost. Nor should trustees suppose that just because their meetings are not frequent the professional will be happy to wait for payment until the next meeting is held.

Relationship between adviser and trustees
It is essential that the individual who advises the trustees commands their respect and trust. All professional relationships require confidence on both sides and in order to be effective the trustees must be able to work with their adviser, discuss the charity's affairs frankly and openly with him or her and take seriously the advice provided.

Effectiveness

Having chosen a professional adviser, it is in the charity's interests that the most effective use should be made of his or her services, both to obtain the best advice for the charity and to avoid wasted costs. For day-to-day contact it is most efficient if there is a single representative of the charity who normally deals directly with the adviser. There will be occasions when a meeting with a group of the trustees (or even with the whole trustee body) is desirable, but this is more useful for general information gathering and background than for more specific points.

A professional should not be presumed to have any more knowledge of the charity and its problems or priorities than the trustees provide. It may, therefore, be sensible to start the relationship with a written summary of the background and, in many cases, a copy of the charity's governing instrument(s) and latest report and statement of accounts. A meeting at an early stage will be helpful to clarify any points which remain in doubt and to consider the precise problem in more detail. There is no reason to assume that an initial consultation should be free of charge. Very often the first meeting with an experienced professional will direct the charity towards the solution.

Communications thereafter will remain of prime importance. The professional will need information from time to time and this should be readily available. Letters and telephone messages should be answered promptly. The professional should also be notified of any relevant changes in the situation and kept informed generally of the charity's progress.

A good working relationship with the charity's professional advisers can be an enormous asset to the charity, but like any other relationship it needs to be nurtured and developed.

Problems with advisers

If there are any problems in the trustees' relationship with the adviser, he or she, or the senior partner in the adviser's firm, should be told at once and action taken to resolve the problems. There is often a simple remedy and there is, of course, no excuse for complaining of poor service only when the invoice arrives.

If, as sometimes happens for a variety of reasons, the trustees reach the conclusion that they will not stay with a particular professional adviser, they should take action to terminate the relationship at once rather than allow the relationship to deteriorate. However, they should remember that it is unlikely that their papers will be returned until they have paid any outstanding fees.

If the worst comes to the worst, the trustees may have to consider taking legal action against a professional for loss caused to the charity through negligence. They will require prompt, independent advice from a solicitor on any such move.

Mistakes to avoid

It is up to the trustees to consult a professional as soon as a problem or potential problem appears. It is not wise to leave the consultation until the trustees have tried, and failed, to solve it themselves, thereby making the situation more complex and difficult to solve. Neither must the trustees simply ignore the problem, hoping that it will go away. Even if a particular difficulty does not materialise, it will be useful to have obtained advice for a future occasion, and the trustees may learn something beneficial to the charity in the course of obtaining the advice.

Trustees should avoid the error of thinking that they know the answer before they have asked the question. Sometimes they will find that they have asked the wrong question and that the answer is not what they had expected. In order to make the most of advice received they should keep an open mind and be prepared to listen as well as to speak.

There are few outcomes more frustrating for a professional person than to give careful, reasoned advice only for it to be ignored for some subjective reason. The occasions on which professional advice should not be followed are rare; such an outcome will usually be a waste of time for all concerned as well as a waste of the charity's money. If the reasons for the advice are not understood, the trustees should request a further, written, explanation.

On the other hand, trustees should not go to the extreme of passing on to a professional adviser the responsibility for deciding an issue of policy which is properly within their discretion. A professional will be an expert in his or her field, but the trustees remain the experts in their charity, and the decision-makers for it.

Particular specialists

Particular types of profession or business have their own requirements and charities should be aware that there may be special considerations or limitations.

Banking, for example, is currently going through a period of rapid change with new technology. It is prudent to discuss how the charity can make the most effective use of the available services, as well as keeping costs to a minimum, and trustees should be willing to consider modifications to the charity's practices (eg by collecting and paying in all donations at a single point) to achieve these ends.

Barristers may only be instructed via another professional person, ie a solicitor or (in an increasing number of cases) by direct professional access through an accountant, surveyor or chartered secretary or other professional authorised to give instructions.

There is a proliferation of para-legal services which may appear more attractive on cost grounds than consulting a solicitor. However, it is worth bearing in mind that charity law is a specialist area which the average licensed conveyancer, for example, may not readily be able to research. Similarly, a design consultant is not the same as an architect.

Charity consultants, including fundraising consultants, of whom there are a great number, do not necessarily have any professional qualification or supervision, although they may belong to the Institute of Charity Fundraising Managers ('ICFM'). Particular care is required when choosing an appropriate consultant and entering into an agreement. It is unwise to commit the charity to a long-term contract. It should also be remembered that consultants should not normally be paid a retainer as opposed to an hourly or daily rate.

Investment advisers must be informed of the charity's investment powers and of the investment policy which the trustees propose to follow. Trustees should not assume that the charity will obtain a better deal by agreeing to pay commission rather than fees and should also be wary of 'hidden extra' charges.

Beauty parades

The expression 'beauty parade' is commonly used in the commercial world to describe a method of choosing between competing professionals by asking them to present what they offer. All professionals are in competition to an extent, but it will not be sensible to use this method of choosing between them unless the charity is able to provide a very clear brief of what it requires. It should also be recognised that unless the charity is looking for the qualities of a good salesman a beauty parade may not disclose the relevant strengths and weaknesses of the competitors. Other methods are simply to enquire carefully and to compare.

Employees and volunteers

For all but the smallest charities, the manpower provided by the trustees alone is not enough. Workers, paid or unpaid, must be recruited. In fact, many of the most prominent and influential people in the charity world today are employees rather than trustees.

Unfortunately, charities in general do not have a good track record in this sphere. Even apart from the effects of the recession, there is a relatively fast turnover among charity employees. One of the reasons for this is simple lack of thought; it need not be so.

In order to attract good people to work for a charity the charity needs to demonstrate that it can provide a satisfactory working environment, something it cannot easily do until it has discovered its own management style.

As usual, the responsibility falls on the trustees. They set the pace, indicate the expectations, decide on the rewards and, as the charity grows, choose the leaders who, in due course, will be doing much of this on their own initiative, and building up the charity's corporate culture and traditions.

It is worth using a little imagination on this topic. From the charity's point of view the work must be done as effectively and efficiently as possible. No one should suppose that working for a charity is an easy option or that competition or its equivalent does not apply. If, however, the workers are looked upon as mere human resources, it is easy to make the mistake of demoralising them by over-work or unrealistic targets, which is likely to result in the opposite of the intended outcome.

Interviewing candidates

Interviewing candidates for positions is a skill which can be learned or which can be bought in especially for the occasion. Some charities have found the specialist recruitment consultancies helpful (see Appendix C), but it is as well if the trustees have given thought to the sorts of qualities, qualifications or skills which they are looking for to carry out the job in hand. In formal terms this is called a person specification.

What, then, do workers need in order to give their best for the optimum length of time? In many cases, working for a charity brings its own reward, in the sense that the job is in itself worth while. That indicates a need to involve workers in the charity's goals and achievements.

Freedom from insecurity

Freedom from insecurity is provided, in the case of employees, by their contract of employment, which is required by law, and, in the case of both employees and volunteers, by coherent and predictable management arrangements. This can be achieved through consultation, discussion, the employee knowing the extent of his or her responsibilities, a sense of belonging and no sudden surprises.

Freedom from annoyance

In this category can be included all the nagging distractions, from bullying and undue bureaucracy to machinery which does not work. A procedure for airing grievances and a method for improving procedures is essential.

Encouragement or praise when deserved

Employees need to be reassured that their efforts are appreciated. Equally, employees need to be told if their work is not up to standard.

Support for weaknesses

Not everyone is good at everything, and people do not always neatly fit the job. A constructive approach enables the jobs to be modified to fit the people. The experience of volunteering shows that this can work with unpaid jobs too.

Training

The possibility of training or of gaining experience to allow for career development, for example specialist courses, secondments, temporary promotions and special assignments may all be considered, but simply allowing a junior member of staff or volunteer to exercise some initiative can prove unexpectedly fruitful.

Fairness

Life may be unfair, but a charity should not be demonstrating that. It is not, in fact, a simple matter to achieve fairness. Goodwill is essential, but there must also be proper job descriptions, systems for appraising jobs and staff, annual reports with built-in checks and balances, an allowance for the differences between people (so that, for example, the loudest voice does not determine priorities) and compliance with race relations and sex discrimination legislation. Charities, generally, do not have such a bad image as some other employers when it comes to ageism.

Remuneration (including pension rights)

Remuneration for employees, should be at, or as near, the going rate for the job as the charity can decently afford. Working for a charity does not remove the material concerns which affect other mortals or diminish family or other responsibilities. Providing housing for employees can be extremely helpful, but it must be borne in mind that the employee will retire in due course and may then wish to have his or her own home.

Health and safety legislation

Health and safety legislation should, of course, be observed, whether the staff are paid or unpaid.

Relationship between director and trustees

The director or chief executive of a substantial charity is in a special position since his or her responsibilities towards the charity mirror those of the trustees themselves, whilst the position affords actual power and control which may exceed that of the trustees. The relationship between the trustees and the director is vitally important. Confidence on both sides is of the first importance, but the director should never be placed in the position of feeling the full weight of responsibility for the charity. He or she must be able to seek guidance, if necessary as a matter of urgency, from the trustees and must be able to look to the trustees to make decisions, particularly decisions on policy. The best ideas and suggestions do not necessarily spring from those who will have to implement them.

Good management

From the management point of view, charities are not very different from other businesses. It is true that charities do not make money for its own sake, but there will always be some way of measuring their success or lack of it, and their activities have very specific financial implications.

This is underlined by the current trend for charities to be invited to tender for services and, thereby, compete with institutions in the private sector or with local or health authorities or, indeed, government departments.

It is wise, as a charity approaches medium size, to take positive steps to plan its management by looking at its resources, actual and potential, its immediate aims and longer-term plans (and the means which are available or which will need to be developed or acquired to achieve them), its philosophy, values and style and how it presents itself.

Planning is by no means enough. Regular reviews and assessments are required and proposals must be placed in an order of priority – and followed up. From time to time, a 'SWOT' analysis is helpful, identifying strengths, weaknesses, opportunities and threats, in order to decide how best to use or cope with them. Sometimes it may be worth examining a perceived weakness to see whether it has any hidden advantages and vice versa. Another strategy is to take a particular activity within the charity, for example information systems, and undertake a thorough review.

Time

Time is generally in short supply: if it is not (and sometimes, of course, if it is) the charity may not be making the best use of it. An annual timetable, with published target dates, can help the charity to avoid last-minute rushes to meet deadlines for such matters as producing the accounts. A policy decision on the time in which letters or applications are answered or whether the unsuccessful applications are to be answered at all, will help to create norms of working and reasonable expectations on the part of applicants and correspondents.

Special care is needed when the charity has outlying groups or branches, or where some of the activities, eg trading or campaigning, have been hived off to separate bodies, which may not themselves be charities.

Coherence

Coherence, in the sense that the organisation should have an inner logic, is necessary to avoid confusion about what people are supposed to be doing. Communication, reporting back and accountability within the whole set-up are essential to avoid confusion about what is actually going on. Whilst there may be good reasons for the same people to be involved in different aspects of activities, care is needed to ensure that the structures are not allowed to become obscure, or unduly complex. The British Legion, which was the subject of a Charity Commission investigation, was criticised for having an over-complicated committee structure in which some people, wearing different hats, were monitoring themselves, and charitable funds were inadvertently being used to support a non-charitable organisation.

Charity consultants

If trustees find that they have inherited a management structure which seems obscure or difficult, or have any reason to be dissatisfied with the arrangement and cannot readily find a solution, it may be worth while to engage the services of a charity consultant or management consultant to investigate, advise and, perhaps, put into place a new system. The National Council for Voluntary Organisations ('NCVO') keeps a list of consultants with details of the services they offer.

Management should not be seen as an end in itself, but always as a means to furthering the charity's purposes in the most effective way. Nor is it something which is 'done' by one group of people to another. It should involve everyone, including the trustees.

Stationery

It may be thought that stationery is unimportant and that the content of what is communicated is the charity's only concern. This is not the attitude of the law.

Every registered charity (with a gross income of £5000 per year or more) is obliged to state the fact that it is a registered charity on all its official documents, including cheques, invoices, receipts and written or printed appeals for funds. It is a punishable offence for a trustee or employee of a charity to authorise the issue of a document which does not comply with this requirement (unless there is a reasonable excuse).

Every limited liability company, charitable or not, is obliged, by company law, to give its full name on all its outgoing documents and, in the case of a charitable company, must state the fact that it is a charity. Non-compliance is an offence.

A charity or a non-charitable body which is registered for VAT should quote its VAT registration number on all invoices and receipts.

These legal requirements can be observed in any reasonable way which the trustees decide, as long as relevant statements are legible and given in English. There is, thus, scope for incorporating them in the design of the stationery and using it to announce or present the charity in a suitable way.

Stationery provides the first direct impression about the charity and its style and values which many people will receive. It will be useful to consider particular points, such as whether the paper should be recycled (reflecting concern with environmental issues), whether there should be a logo or script which will give some idea of the charity's purpose or philosophy in encapsulated form, and how much information, for example about patrons, staff or trustees, should be provided on the notepaper (bearing in mind that such details can change).

If the charity provides a service which is of financial value, or even if it merely wishes its work to be identifiable, it is worth considering registration of the design or logo as a service mark at the Trade Marks Registry. A solicitor, patent agent or trade mark agent can be engaged to advise on and make the application, but it is also possible to apply direct, and official guidance is provided.

Cost

The cost of stationery is a major constraint and, again, can be used positively to indicate the charity's concern for economy. It is, in any case, an inexcusable extravagance to use expensive, printed or high-quality stationery for internal paperwork.

The paperwork used for seeking funds needs special attention, and may differ according to the person or body to whom it is addressed. Commercially popular, 'glossy' brochures will not necessarily convey the message that the charity needs (as opposed to spends) money. Unduly lengthy and detailed submissions or those which are very closely typed, are not likely to be read in full. A naïvely organised piece of writing will risk conveying the message that funds will also be organised naïvely.

Computers

These days, no mention of stationery is complete without reference to the ubiquitous computer. Computers, wordprocessors and desk-top publishing are capable of transforming a charity's efficiency, by cutting out labour-intensive routines. Just as easily, however, they can lead to considerable problems, frustrations and consequential expense. No one is immune from making mistakes, particularly in a rapidly developing field. It is well worth seeking advice, not only from suppliers but also from other organisations performing comparable tasks, before acquiring the equipment or software, and arranging for appropriate training.

Premises

A charity which is a limited company or friendly or industrial and provident society must have a registered office, clearly marked as such. However, there is no need for a charity to have its own office or premises and, in fact, many small charities, and some larger, grant-making charities, are administered from the homes of the trustees or the director or from the place of work of a part-time clerk or secretary.

Charities whose work involves the use of land or buildings, or who employ a number of members of staff (or volunteers) all working together, however, need their own premises. These may be owned freehold or leased or rented or, in some cases, held on a contractual licence which does not amount to a tenancy. They may be used exclusively by the charity or shared with other organisations, including, sometimes, other charities.

Appearance of premises

Where the premises are used for the functional purposes of the charity, eg as a college or hospital or church or veterinary clinic, the functional use will determine the way the accommodation is arranged and will influence the appearance of the building. There can be no better (and no worse) advertisement for the charity than the outside of its functional property (and the interior too, if it is open to the public). It may become a landmark in the district, and it is to be hoped that it will not be an eye-sore. It should also be considered whether the site and building are suitable for the practical requirements of the charity.

Where the premises are the charity's headquarters or office, rather than being directly used to deliver a service to beneficiaries in person, their external appearance and internal functioning are equally important. Like stationery, they give a message to the world at large about the charity's values and approach to its work. In this case, however, the message tends to be a continuing and often permanent one which would be difficult or expensive to alter drastically.

The right sort of message will be conveyed if the approach to the premises is clearly signposted, the entrance accessible (to the disabled as well as the able-bodied) and is neither scruffy nor too imposing. If there are reception arrangements these should put visitors at their ease and, perhaps, include posters, leaflets or other materials which illustrate the charity's work and priorities.

Regulations

Trustees and officers should take care to ensure that they are aware of and comply with all the various regulations regarding the use of office and other buildings and any proposed alterations to them, for example fire regulations, health and safety regulations, building regulations and planning permissions.

Problems foreseen are often avoided, and one of the essentials is to provide staff with clear instructions about what to do in the event of fire or other emergencies. Policy decisions on eating, drinking and smoking in the building are helpful: a straightforward ban, which should of course be observed scrupulously by the trustees as well as by staff and visitors, can be the simplest solution.

Listed buildings

Many charities work from listed buildings, which may provide a pleasant, general environment but prove difficult to adapt as the charity expands (in view of the conflict between modern safety standards and the conservation interest). Security from theft or damage is also increasingly necessary, and may be difficult to reconcile with other desiderata. Adaptations or special arrangements may be required where sensitive equipment is installed.

Moving premises

Moving premises, eg when a charity acquires its own premises for the first time, or when it decides to move to a different or cheaper location, brings its own opportunities and risks. Simple precautions, such as notifying regular contacts of the proposed change of address, should be planned well in advance and may provide a good occasion for a wider and more general mailshot.

Budgeting for the new premises is essential and in this process the longer-term, as well as the shorter-term, should be considered. For example, questions to be raised could be as follows. Should a reserve fund for future repairs and decorations be set up from the start? Will the existing equipment be sufficient? Will the new location enable savings to be made on incidental costs, for example can staff be recruited locally, saving on season ticket loans?

Neighbours

It is also useful to research the local services and facilities and to consider whether savings could be achieved or efficiency increased by co-operating with neighbours. It is most important that a charity should have good relations with its neighbours. Like any other business or resident, a charity is part of the local community and will be noticed and talked about. Good relations are vital where the activity of the charity is likely to cause concern to those living or working close by and who are not well-informed about how the charity operates. People who take the 'not in my backyard' approach and who object to activities they fear, can often be pacified by a patient explanation of the purpose of the work, whether it is rehabilitation of drug users or the keeping of donkeys, and of the safeguards which the planners (presumably) have thought sufficient.

Training

For some groups of people, regular training courses are taken for granted as a normal part of working life. For others, training does not seem relevant. For the latter group, training of the type given on a formal course may not be appropriate. However, there will undoubtedly be other forms of learning which they would welcome and enjoy. Included under the heading of 'training' for the purposes of this book are methods of learning connected directly or indirectly with the work of a charity.

Many trustees, employees and advisers of charities will have undergone professional or vocational training as part of their education. Most professions now require active members to undergo 'continuing education' to keep themselves up to date in a wide choice of subjects, some of which are very specialised. As a matter of interest, such formal courses include charity law for solicitors.

Self-help

In addition, training opportunities exist through self-help through an association. For example, a lawyer who is interested may join the Association of Charity Lawyers or the Society of Trust and Estate Practitioners, and attend sociable meetings at which talks will be given. A Chartered Secretary may join the Charity Group of the Institute of Chartered Secretaries and Administrators, which provides much the same benefits. A charity accountant may join the influential Charity Finance Directors' Group. Management training, as already noted, is widely available, whether at vast expense and prestige or through local authority courses for the voluntary sector or at some intermediate level or cost. Some so-called management courses are, unfortunately, eccentric or experimental and should not be tried by those of a nervous disposition. It is often better to start by joining an association of people performing similar work functions and decide, after discussion of the experiences of others, what course would be most suitable for an individual.

Academic institutions

Academic institutions are increasingly moving into the area of training for work with charities. For example, the South Bank University in London has pioneered an MSc course in charity finance, and Exeter University includes a charities option in its MBA course.

Technical skills training

Training in technical skills is readily available at all levels of computing, word-processing and other uses of information technology. In such a rapidly changing field, it is difficult for people honestly to claim that they know it all already.

Special courses

There are also courses designed with very particular types of students in mind, for example self-assertion for women.

Opportunities for staff

A good employer will encourage staff to undertake training courses whether by offering study leave or providing in-house training, but to make this worth while it is essential that the employee is given credit for the training undertaken and asked to make use of it. Charities need to have a policy on training.

One of the problems faced by junior staff or certain specialists is that they are categorised when they enter the charity's service and, in reality, have no opportunity of career development or diversification, except by leaving to go to another job. This is extremely wasteful of the very people whom a charity should be retaining and developing. It accords with the flexible spirit of most charities that such employees should be given better opportunities.

Internal training

Apart from formal training courses and organised professional activities there is a great deal of activity, within the charity world, in the sphere of informal learning through meetings and discussions. These can be of inestimable benefit not only to the participants themselves, whose problems at work will fall into perspective when compared with the experience of other people in similar posts, but also to the charity itself. Often at minimal cost, and during a lunch hour or in the early evening, those involved in running a charity can imbibe new ideas, gain in morale and bring back to the charity a sense of being part of a larger movement and of being near the forefront of the thinking within it.

Most of these meetings and discussions are advertised regularly by the NCVO or elsewhere in the charity press, and are attended not only by charity workers but also by trustees. There are many reasons why trustees should make more efforts to attend such meetings, both to learn and to contribute.

Following a small survey, which led to the announcement that a large proportion of charity trustees did not even know that they were trustees, the NCVO has established a Trustee Training Unit, especially to help trustees to appreciate their responsibilities.

In-house training may sound more mundane, but there is certainly a place for a period of induction for new trustees, staff and volunteers, and there is no reason why these should not be combined to give the newcomers a chance to meet one another. There is also an advantage in getting staff and trustees together for conferences or meetings, or merely for social events, from time to time. In addition, there may be scope for specialist training where the charity operates an institution, performs an unusual function, or has particular traditions which involve special ways of doing things.

For some charities, it may be economical, and provide additional interest for participants, to arrange a combined training activity with another charity, or another branch of the same charity, or with another organisation in the locality.

Learning and training should be an enjoyable, positive experience. It is, therefore, desirable to seek the best training available. On the other hand, it has cost implications and charities must be wary of extravagance. A constructive approach is to regard the cost as equivalent to an investment and to be careful both about initial selection and monitoring and utilising the service which has been provided.

Troubleshooting

No charity, however well run, is immune from the occasional disaster or hitch. The importance lies in what is done about it and what is learned from it. Sometimes, the action taken determines whether or not the charity survives; at other times, it is the reduction in the amount by which the charity's credibility is damaged. Loss of credibility does not only mean loss of potential for fundraising; it can also make it difficult to recruit good staff or trustees or to be taken seriously by the authorities and others whom the charity wishes to reach.

Physical emergencies

Physical emergencies can be dealt with by practical steps, for example by having well-thought-out procedures to deal with fire or flood, and adequate insurance cover.

Insurance

Insurance will also go some way to assist in the case of financial loss through negligence or theft or other dishonesty on the part of members of staff, although careful selection procedures, including the taking up of references and prudent financial management which avoids putting temptation in people's way, is preferable and usually effective.

Negligence

Losses caused by the negligence of advisers or other independent contractors should be recoverable from their professional indemnity insurers, if necessary through court action. This is one of the arguments in favour of appointing a surveyor or architect to supervise work on a building project.

Tenants' defaults

The defaults of tenants who are not beneficiaries of the charity can be guarded against by taking adequate deposits on the grant of the tenancy, making sure that there is an effective system for collecting rent and investigating every suspected breach of covenant.

Compensation

Failures by suppliers or service-providers can be dealt with by a claim for compensation. Similarly, if a trustee wanders off the straight and narrow and commits a breach of trust, prompt action, if necessary through the courts, will often provide the best solution.

Problems

Troubleshooting is less straightforward in three sets of circumstances.

1 Running out of money

A charity which has made plans on the strength of promises of money which do not materialise may find it impossible to continue to operate on anything like the scale it envisaged, and may be forced to make staff redundant or even to wind up the charity. In the case of a charitable company, the charity trustees will be personally at risk of having to pay the charity's debts if they allow it to continue operating while it is technically insolvent (ie cannot pay its debts from its assets). It *must*, therefore, stop operations.

It is wise to cease operating in such circumstances even where company law does not provide this incentive. It is then up to the trustees to take urgent steps either to find the required funds or to reorganise the charity's work in a way which is practicable. It may involve a radical alteration to the constitution or functions of the charity, or amalgamation with a similar charity, or even a takeover by another body of trustees.

If a charity is vulnerable through dependence on grant aid the staff must be made aware of this, and sufficient financial advice should be obtained in order that staff and beneficiaries may be protected as far as possible. This is also another very good reason for maintaining co-operative relationships with other bodies.

2 Charity Commission Inquiry

Anyone may make a complaint about a particular charity to the Charity Commissioners, who now have the staff and resources to investigate any complaint which is well-founded and does not refer to an exempt charity.

There are other bodies (such as the Housing Corporation) which will investigate complaints against specific types of exempt charity.

The Commissioners have a number of wide-ranging powers to protect the assets of a charity which is under investigation and may, for example, obtain information and documents, order a professional audit, suspend trustees and officers, freeze bank accounts and prevent transactions with the charity even before their investigation is complete. Subsequently, they may decide to remove one or more of the trustees or officers, appoint new trustees, appoint a receiver and manager to run the charity or even transfer the assets to another charity and wind up the original charity (in the case of a charitable company, they petition the court to do so). Further, the Commissioners or the Attorney-General may decide to bring legal proceedings against one or more of the trustees, seeking to make them personally liable for the damage to the charity.

A recent relaxation in the confidentiality principles allows the Inland Revenue, the Customs and Excise Department, rating authorities and others to share their information with the Commissioners when there is reason to suspect abuse.

Although a large proportion of complaints which are investigated ultimately prove unfounded, the fact that a charity is being investigated, which is frequently of interest to the press, grant-makers and others, tends to indicate that something is wrong with the charity or its administration and this, in itself, can be very damaging.

To avoid uncalled for complaints, charity trustees should, first, take care not to do anything which would allow staff, tenants, advisers or beneficiaries to feel that they have been unfairly treated and internal complaints procedures should be established to deal with such problems. Regrettably, there are occasions when the director or other senior staff member has become alienated from the trustees and, despite the risk to his or her job, will take a perceived problem to the Commissioners instead of consulting the trustees. Secondly, it is prudent to establish good relationships with the press, by providing ample information and responding helpfully when asked.

If a serious complaint is made or a formal investigation is proposed, one of the most constructive responses, which will generally be welcomed by the Commissioners, is for the charity to set up its own inquiry to establish the facts and correct and learn from any mistakes which have been made. This is not only very helpful and positive in itself, but enables any press reports to sound positive also, and underlines the fact that the trustees are in charge (not the disaster).

3 Mediation

It is a regettable fact that many charities suffer, from time to time, from internal disputes, either within the workforce or the trustee body or between one and the other. There is no reasonable excuse for such self-defeating and destructive behaviour, which fits no one's idea of charity.

Publicity is extremely damaging in this situation, both because it encourages attitudes to harden and because of its effect on the charity's public image.

Good management, open communications, the careful selection of trustees and staff, a strong sense of commitment and agreed priorities, will all help to guard against this kind of calamity. If it does arise, however, feelings are likely to run high, righteous indignation flourishes and intemperate words appear in print.

The best solution is not to complain of maladministration to the Charity Commissioners (although they may sometimes be able to suggest a solution) or to resort to litigation (although for some disputes this can appear to be the only way to decide the matter) but to try to resolve the matter amicably in the interests of the charity by negotiation or other means.

A recent development is the use of alternative dispute resolution ('ADR'), a series of techniques aiming to find solutions without litigation. Arbitration is one method, but tends to be costly. Another, less expensive and, in many ways, more satisfactory technique is mediation. A mediator, preferably someone who has been trained in the technique, and who may be nominated by an independent outside agency, is appointed to assist the parties to reach a solution by agreement. The mediator's fees are paid equally by both sides to ensure impartiality. The process is not binding unless and until an agreement is reached. The mediator will not impose the solution but try to bring out the underlying common ground between the parties and discover in what ways the matters which they regard as most important can be incorporated into the solution. Most mediations result in a final, binding agreement, and those which do not often make the remaining stages in the dispute simpler and easier to deal with.

Chapter 5
EUROPE

How charities fit in

There are equivalents of charities in other European countries, but since their legal systems are based on Roman Law, which did not have the need to develop the trust concept or the concept of charitable purposes, English Law stands out as having the most developed legal concept of charity and the most refined methods of supervision and accountability. In relation to what we recognise as charities, the technical form of the organisation is far more important in Europe than in this country. In Europe, two main categories are prevalent: Foundations, which are similar to UK charitable trusts but have a corporate form; and Associations, which are similar to what would be called voluntary organisations in the UK. In addition, churches in Europe carry out a good deal of charitable work directly.

The European Community has only recently begun to come to grips with the voluntary sector in general. For many years it was regarded as having little relevance to the European economy and outside (what used to be called) the Common Market. That view has been modified with the recognition that 'not-for-profit' bodies have an effect on the economy as users and providers of services, that social questions are highly relevant to economic results and that the voluntary sector has grown and continues to do so. As a result, the expression 'social economy' or 'l'économie sociale' has been coined.

Social economy

The social economy covers much more than charitable purposes or organisations. It includes non-charitable friendly societies, agricultural co-operatives and other mutual trading bodies, housing associations and what is known as 'social tourism', ie the provision of holidays for workers or for the poor. Such organisations may operate in commercial ways, except that their aim is not profit but the benefit of members or a section of the public. They are sometimes designated, in French, organisations 'sans but lucratif', a phrase which is closer in meaning to 'non-profit-distributing', or the American phrase 'not-for-profit' than to the usually inexact 'non-profit-making'.

At present, Europe-wide regulation of the social economy is in inchoate form, and it may be many years before decisions are taken and implemented either to harmonise the rules (including supervision on the one hand and tax reliefs on the other) between Member States or, bearing in mind the emergence of the principle of subsidiarity, the decision is taken to leave most of these matters to individual States to regulate in accordance with their national cultural traditions. On the other hand, the issue of whether, and if so how, to operate in other European countries and to tap European sources of funds, will be of increasing relevance to charities which are not purely local (and even to some which are) as the European Community encroaches on more aspects of life.

European Community law

As a result of being a signatory to the European Treaties, the UK is subject to Community law, which must be applied by UK courts. There are, however, different kinds of Community legislation which affect us in different ways.

Treaties

The treaties, which may be amended and supplemented from time to time, are the primary legislation and directly applicable to governments and commercial (and other) entities. They define the areas of policy for which the Community is responsible and set out general principles, for example on competition, which can have a direct effect on the way economic activities operate.

Regulations

Regulations are binding, unavoidable and directly applicable in the courts of all Member States.

Directives

Directives are addressed to national governments and require them to introduce domestic legislation to achieve a stated result. The method of achieving the stated result is for the Member State concerned. They are, naturally, less detailed than regulations and deal with policy. However, they are binding on the Member States, who must report what steps have been taken to implement them and do so by a stated date.

Decisions

Decisions are addressed to particular States, institutions or individuals, on whom they are binding.

Recommendations and Opinions

Recommendations and Opinions are not binding but, nevertheless, carry considerable weight, and may be referred to in decisions of the European Court of Justice.

The following summary of the European institutions explains by which of the institutions the foregoing expressions of the authority of the Community are made.

European institutions

There is an interlocking series of institutions which carry out the functions of the Community in ways which are still being refined and developed.

Council of Ministers

The Council of Ministers is the principal legislative assembly and, whilst it was originally intended to legislate only on proposals from the Commission (see below), it has taken on the role of initiating policy. This is of particular relevance in enlarging the scope of Community policy where the subject is not clearly covered by the treaties. The composition of the Council depends on the question at issue. Thus, at a General Council meeting the Foreign Ministers of Member States will be present, whereas more specialised ministers will attend meetings of the Technical Councils, dealing with such matters as agriculture. The President of the Council of Ministers is often referred to as the President of the Community, a post which is held by Member States, in turn, for six months at a time, and enables the holder to set the agenda.

Committees of Permanent Representatives

Preparatory work for meetings of the Council of Ministers is carried out by one of the Committees of Permanent Representatives (COREPERS 1 and 2) and, below them, by a number of committees and working parties which advise the Council and Commission and analyse Commission proposals. There is also an informal group of committees advising on policy areas which are not formally covered by the treaties.

European Council

The European Council is not provided for under the treaties but has developed in response to a need. It consists of the heads of government of

the Member States and the heads of the Commission, who aim to set goals
and make policy decisions (sometimes on specific issues), consider the admission of new members to the Community, resolve internal problems and deal
with challenges which face the Community from outside. Meetings are held
at least every six months.

Commission

The Commission is often described as the Civil Service of the Community
but, whilst it has equivalent functions, it has greater influence and power to
initiate policy than a Government Department in the UK. It is headed by 17
Commissioners, each with responsibility for a particular area of policy allocated by the President of the Commission, who is appointed by the European
Council. Each Commissioner is supported by a 'cabinet' of officials, usually
from his or her own State.

Directorates General

Below the Commissioners are the Directorates General, whose responsibilities
are concerned with different areas of policy. The social economy (see p 67
above) comes under Directorate General 23 (usually referred to as DG
XXIII), a small DG with only two directorates and no divisions within it.

There have been problems when issues cut across the policy areas of more
than one DG which have affected those in the voluntary sector. A consultative
process is now being considered to ensure that the Commission takes account
of the effects on charities and kindred bodies when drawing up legislation.
The functions of the Commission, of most concern to charities, are described
under 'Interaction' at p 72 below.

European Parliament

The European Parliament is a directly elected assembly whose members sit for
terms of five years. At present there are 518 MEPs. Members gravitate to various groups, according to their national party, the most prominent of which are
the European People's Party (roughly 'Christian Democrat') and the Socialist
Group. There is also the Group of the Greens and the Group for the European
Unitarian Left. The procedural arrangements make provision for represen-
tation of the various groupings, both in plenary sessions and in committees.

The plenary sessions take place in Strasbourg and the committees meet in
Brussels. The secretariat is based in Luxembourg, where the library is situated. Researchers and parliamentary staff make use of the library for information on social issues, to which charities may usefully contribute material.

Committees

The committees carry out most of the work of the Parliament. There are 18 permanent committees and several ad hoc committees which are formed to consider specific issues. The concerns of charities are not covered by any one committee but are distributed between several, including the standing committees for Social Affairs, Employment and the Working Environment and for Agriculture, Fisheries and Rural Development. The committees examine proposals from the Commission on which the opinion of Parliament is sought, and each is led by a 'rapporteur'.

The main functions of the European Parliament are the consideration of proposed legislation and, most importantly, the setting of the budget. The European Parliament is able to suggest amendments to legislative proposals and to add new areas of expenditure to the budget. If, when so doing, it oversteps the limits of the areas for which there is formal authority to operate, it is understood that the Commission and the Council of Ministers will provide the necessary authority. Areas of particular interest to charities are mentioned under 'Interaction' at p 72 below.

Economic and Social Committee

The Economic and Social Committee consists of 89 members chosen by the governments of Member States and representing three main groups – employers, workers and others (including environmental protection agencies, the professions, small businesses, consumers and local authorities). This committee was established because it was considered that the European Parliament did not provide enough scope for the discussion of these specific interests. The Committee is divided into nine sections, dealing, for example, with the environment, public health, social issues, family issues and educational and cultural matters. There is a plenary session in Brussels 10 or 12 times per year, and the Committee gives influential Opinions, prepared by rapporteurs after careful consultation, on Community affairs.

Referral of a question to the Committee for its Opinion is sometimes compulsory, as when it concerns social policy or the European Social Fund, but is otherwise optional. The Committee may also give an Opinion on its own initiative.

Committee of the Regions

A new committee, entitled the Committee of the Regions, has been proposed, following the Maastricht Treaty, to represent regional interests.

**European Foundation for the Improvement of Living and
Working Conditions**

The European Foundation for the Improvement of Living and Working
Conditions, usually called the European Foundation, meets in Dublin. Its
members represent employers, trade unions and governments. The Foundation produces detailed reports on major issues, including, for example, housing projects for the young and counselling for the long-term unemployed,
and also holds conferences on particular themes.

Council of Europe

The Council of Europe is not an institution of the European Community but
was set up after the Second World War to safeguard the cultural heritage of
the European peoples, especially respect for human rights and the rule of law
by democratic institutions, and to encourage social and economic progress.

It consists of a Committee of Ministers and a Parliamentary Assembly,
both drawn from the democratic institutions in European countries, and a
Standing Conference of Local and Regional Authorities. It was the first body
in Europe to recognise the need for consultation arrangements for Non-
Governmental Organisations ('NGOs') (see p 73 below).

Interaction

It can truly be said that making positive use of the European institutions and
obtaining grants from them is an art in itself. The following may help to
indicate areas which are worth exploring.

The Commission

To influence Community legislation and the adoption of new policies the best
approach may be via the Commission, which, in formulating legislative and
policy proposals, has a healthy tradition of consulting people and organisations which have expertise in the subject, and setting up committees for this
purpose. There is a proposal to set up a consultative committee on the social
economy, which would be an obvious route for many charities which wish
to present their viewpoint.

The Commission also monitors Community policy and supervises its
implementation, by making decisions, regulations and directives, ensuring
consistency and collecting (and spending) revenue (eg VAT). There are two
'structural funds' of particular relevance to charities, from which it is possible

to obtain grant aid. The European Social Fund and the European Regional Development Fund operate in a co-ordinated way to achieve five aims: developing backward regions; changing declining industrial areas; integrating the young into the job market; dealing with long-term unemployment; and developing rural areas.

The Commission shares with the European Court of Justice the role of ensuring compliance with Community legislation, for example failures on the part of national governments to implement directives.

The European Parliament

As indicated above, the European Parliament is a true debating assembly and not a legislature. Its major decision-making concerns the budget. Indirect influence through the library at Luxembourg has already been mentioned (see p 70 above).

It is also possible to influence ultimate decision-making by persuading an MEP to suggest amendments to proposed legislation which comes to the Parliament for its opinion before being laid before the Council of Ministers. Less commonly, the Parliament is given the opportunity of the equivalent of a second reading of a proposal after the Council of Ministers has considered it, or may be consulted on a policy issue even before a proposal is formulated.

The European Social Committee

The European Social Committee is not a decision-making body, but it does exercise a serious influence on policy and may be persuaded to recruit expert advisers from charities operating in the field which it is considering, or to incorporate, in its reports, information or materials produced by relevant charities.

The European Foundation

Similar influences may be possible in relation to Foundation reports. Attendance at a conference may also prove very helpful in establishing contacts for the charity with others concerned with similar problems.

The Council of Europe

The work of the Council of Europe with Non-Governmental Organisations ('NGOs') has led to increased influence for these bodies, which must be international. They can apply to be consulted in any of nine fields, including health, youth, heritage and the environment and human rights, and act as advisers to the Council or its committees and through various NGO meetings and networks. A charity which is not itself an international body can gain influence indirectly through one which is.

European Programmes

In addition to the European Foundation there is another permanent agency, the European Centre for Vocational Training ('CEDEFOP') which is relevant to the work of some charities.

Besides these permanent groups there is a series of short-term programmes in the field of social policy, which provide either funds or information and advice, or a combination, and report back to the DG by which they were established. The programmes are operated through existing outside agencies, many of which have advisory committees which provide another avenue of influence for interested charities.

Among these programmes are specialised regional or local networks combating poverty, which have been in existence with more or less similar aims since the 1970s. Charities are usually closely involved with such work, and efforts are made by means of research projects and otherwise to build on the experience gained and pass on the lessons learned. There is a research project based at the Local Government Centre of the Warwick Business School which supports the programme in the UK. The central control is based in Lille, France and there is a liaison committee between the Commission and the national governments which, in the UK, includes a representative from the Department of Social Security.

Networks and umbrella bodies

There is an enormous proliferation of networking bodies which operate throughout Europe and, for most charities, they provide the ideal way to examine ways of both operating directly and gaining useful knowledge from other European countries.

The NCVO in the UK provides very practical guidance on how and with whom to make contact, how to apply for grant aid, and aims to act as the spokesman, both in Europe and in Westminster and Whitehall, for the voluntary sector generally.

The Comité Européen des Associations d'intérêt Général ('CEDAG') is a network emanating originally from the Council of Europe, which is leading moves for more formal arrangements within the Community for consultation with charities and other voluntary bodies. There is a proposed European Association Statute on which CEDAG is in discussion with the Commission, via DG XXIII (see p 70 above). In addition, CEDAG uses its influence to press for funding for charitable work and has helped to establish an interest group for the sector (known as an intergroup) within the European Parliament.

The European Foundation Centre ('EFC') represents grant-making bodies across Europe and has links with the Association of Charitable Foundations in the UK and, less directly, with the Council on Foundations in the USA.

The International Society for Third Sector Research ('ISTR') has recently been established to promote academic research and teaching concerning 'the Third, Voluntary or Non-profit Sector' on an international basis.

Appendices

Appendix A: Forms

1. Declaration of Trust

Stamp: 50p

THIS DECLARATION OF TRUST made the [date] by
(1)   [name and address]
(2)   [name and address]
(3)   [name and address]
(4)   [name and address] and
(5)   [name and address] ("the First Trustees")
WITNESSES AS FOLLOWS

1.   INTRODUCTION

   (1)   [Name and address] ("the Founder") desires to establish a
          charitable trust ("the Charity") and to this end has paid the sum of
          £.... to the First Trustees
   (2)   It is envisaged that further sums of money or other property will be
          given to the Charity from time to time

2.   NAME OF CHARITY

The Charity shall be called the [Name] or such other name as the Trustees
from time to time by resolution decide

3.   OBJECTS OF CHARITY

The objects of the Charity are [charitable purposes]

4.   TRUST
The first Trustees and their successors as Trustees of the Charity shall hold
the said sum of £.... and all other money or property which may come into
their hands as such Trustees upon trust to apply [the same without
distinction between capital and income] [the clear income thereof] in
furtherance of the objects

5. POWERS

The Trustees shall have the following powers exercisable in furtherance of the objects:

(1) To employ a clerk and other staff
(2) To acquire property of any kind
(3) To dispose of property (subject to any consents required by law)
(4) To borrow money with or without security (subject to any consents required by law)
(5) To raise funds by any lawful means except permanent trading
(6) To accept gifts for the general purposes of the Charity or for any special purpose within the objects
(7) To establish and maintain a reserve fund to meet planned future expenditure
(8) To invest funds in any lawful manner provided that whenever the amount available to be invested exceeds £5,000 the Trustees must obtain professional advice from a person or firm reasonably believed by them to be experienced in matters of investment
(9) To do anything else within the law which is required in carrying out the objects

6. TRUSTEES

(1) The number of Trustees when complete shall be at least three and not more than seven
(2) [Two] of the Trustees shall be appointed by [names of outside bodies] [and the remaining] Trustees shall be appointed by resolution of the Trustees after consultation with the Founder during the Founder's lifetime [and with . . .]
(3) Every Trustee shall be appointed for a term of office not exceeding three years and may be reappointed [once]
(4) A Trustee's appointment will automatically come to an end in any of the following circumstances:
 (i) If the Trustee concerned sends written notice of resignation to the other Trustees or their clerk
 (ii) If the Trustee concerned is disqualified from acting as a charity trustee
 (iii) If the Trustee concerned is physically or mentally incapable of acting
 (iv) If the Trustee concerned attends no meetings of the Trustees for twelve consecutive months

7. ADMINISTRATION

(1) The Trustees must hold at least two meetings per year
(2) A quorum at meetings of the Trustees shall be [three]
(3) The Trustees must keep a record of their meetings and proceedings and provide for the safe keeping of documents
(4) The Trustees may delegate any of their functions to a committee consisting of at least two of themselves [with power to co-opt] but all acts and proceedings of committees must be reported promptly to the Trustees
(5) The Trustees may delegate the management of the investments belonging to the Charity to professional investment managers who are registered or exempted persons under the Financial Services Act 1986 Provided that the Trustees enter into a written agreement with such managers which includes the following provisions:
  (i) The Trustees may terminate the agreement at any time without notice
  (ii) The Investment Managers must follow the investment policy guidance provided by the Trustees from time to time
  (iii) All transactions must be reported promptly to the Trustees
  (iv) The arrangements must be reviewed at least once in every calendar year.
(6) The Trustees must maintain a bank or building society account in the name of the Charity which must not be operated without the signatures of at least two of the Trustees
(7) The Trustees may from time to time make rules consistent with this Deed to govern their procedures

8. RESTRICTIONS

Money or other property belonging to the Charity must not be used for the following purposes:
(1) Making payment for goods or services or providing any other personal benefit to the Founder, any spouse of the Founder, any Trustee or any member of the immediate family of a Trustee (but there shall be no objection to the use of such money in reimbursing the reasonable out of pocket expenses of Trustees or members of their families [or in paying reasonable remuneration to not more than one of the Trustees being a professional person for work on behalf of the Charity carried out by him or her in a professional capacity on the express instructions of his or her co-

Trustees Provided that the Trustee concerned takes no part in deciding the amount of that remuneration]

(2) In the reduction of benefits provided to any person or locality from rates, taxes or other public funds (but there shall be no objection to the use of such money in supplementing any statutory provision)

9. VARIATION

The provisions of this Deed may be varied at any time by supplemental deed but no variation will be valid if it would [alter the objects of the Charity or this clause or] cause the Charity to lose its charitable status

10. DISSOLUTION

(1) The Trustees may at any time by resolution dissolve the Charity

(2) In the event of a dissolution the Trustees shall be responsible for the orderly winding up of the affairs of the Charity

(3) Any money or property held for the general purposes of the Charity which remains after all debts and liabilities of the Charity have been met must be paid or transferred to another charity or charities having objects similar to the objects of the Charity or applied directly for charitable purposes within those objects

(4) Any property held by the Trustees which is subject to special trusts must be dealt with in accordance with those trusts.

IN WITNESS whereof the parties have executed this deed

SIGNED AS A DEED AND DELIVERED BY

(signatures and witnesses)

2. Constitution of a Charitable Unincorporated Association

1. NAME

The Name of the Association is . . . . . ("The Association")

2. OBJECTS

The Objects of the Association are [charitable objects] ("the Objects")

3. POWERS

In furtherance of the Objects but not otherwise the Association may:
- 3.1 [Special powers linked with the Association eg running a school, carrying out research, publishing a journal etc]
- 3.2 Employ and remunerate staff;
- 3.3 Acquire and dispose of property (subject to any consents required by law);
- 3.4 Invest funds in any lawful manner provided that professional investment advice is obtained whenever it is prudent to do so;
- 3.5 Borrow money without or without giving security (subject to any consents required by law);
- 3.6 Raise funds by any lawful means except permanent trading;
- 3.7 Accept gifts either for the general purposes of the Association or for a specific purpose within or connected with the Objects;
- 3.8 Do anything else within the law which is necessary in carrying out the Objects.

4. MEMBERSHIP

- 4.1 Membership of the Association is open to any individual or organisation who is interested in furthering the Objects and who completes an application form as prescribed by the Executive Committee.
- 4.2 Every member must pay an annual subscription of such amount as the Executive Committee decides from time to time.
- 4.3 Every individual member and the appointed representative of every organisation in membership has one vote at General Meetings of the Association.
- 4.4 A member may resign his, her or its membership at any time and

a member who is three months in arrears with his, her or its subscription is deemed to have resigned but may rejoin on payment of the arrears

4.5   If the Executive Committee consider that a member's conduct is harmful to the Association it may by resolution require the member concerned either to resign or to put his, her or its case to a meeting of the Executive Committee.

4.6   Where the Executive Committee is satisfied after hearing the case put by or on behalf of the member concerned that the member should leave the Association it may terminate that membership by written notice and that notice is final.

4.7   The Executive Committee may make provision for non-voting categories of membership including junior membership, associate membership and honorary membership, and set the subscriptions payable (if any).

4.8   The Executive Committee must keep a list of members in each category.

5. GENERAL MEETINGS

5.1   There must be an Annual General Meeting of the members of the Association once in every calendar year.

5.2   At the Annual General Meeting the members will
5.2.1   Receive the Executive Committee's report for the previous year;
5.2.2   Receive the Treasurer's report and accounts for the previous year;
5.2.3   Elect the Executive Committee for the following year;
5.2.4   Discuss and advise the new Executive Committee on matters of policy for the Association;
5.2.5   Determine any other matter of which notice has been given.

5.3   A Special Meeting of the members of the Association may be held at any time if called by the Executive Committee or if at least [10] members of the Association make a written request to the Executive Committee.

5.4   A Special General Meeting must be called within two weeks of such a request.

5.5   A General Meeting requires 28 days' notice to be given to the members specifying the matters to be dealt with.

5.6   A quorum at a General Meeting is [15] members present in person or a minimum of one third of the membership whichever is the smaller number. If there is no quorum the meeting may be adjourned for at least 14 days and the number present at the adjourned meeting if at least three will constitute a quorum for that meeting.

5.7 The Chairman of the Executive Committee or in his absence some other person elected by the meeting takes the chair at General Meetings.

5.8 Except where this constitution provides for a larger majority on a specific question, every question is decided by a majority of the votes cast. In the case of equality of votes the Chairman has a second or casting vote.

6. EXECUTIVE COMMITTEE: COMPOSITION

6.1 The Executive Committee ("the Committee") is the body responsible for the management of the Association.

6.2 The Committee consists of a minimum of [three] and a maximum of [seven] individuals who are either members of the Association or the appointed representatives of organisations in membership.

6.3 The members of the Committee are elected annually at the Annual General Meeting and normally hold office until the end of the Annual General Meeting the following year.

6.4 Any member of the Committee who resigns by written notice to the Committee, who is absent from three consecutive meetings of the Committee or who is disqualified by law from acting as a charity trustee, ceases automatically to be a member of the Committee.

6.5 Casual vacancies in the Committee may be filled by the Committee by co-option, and a co-opted member will have the same voting powers and hold office for the same period as the Committee member he or she replaces.

7. EXECUTIVE COMMITTEE: PROCEDURES

7.1 The Committee must meet at least [four] times in every calendar year. A special meeting of the Committee may be called at any time on [seven] days' notice. A quorum at Committee meetings is [three].

7.2 At the first meeting of the Committee in every year the members must appoint from among themselves a Chairman, a Treasurer and such other honorary officers as they think fit.

7.3 Every question is decided by a simple majority of the Committee members present and voting at a meeting. In the case of equality of votes the Chairman of the meeting has a second or casting vote.

7.4 The Committee may appoint sub-committees to advise them or to carry out specific tasks in the management of the Association but sub-committees must always report back to the Committee as soon as possible.

7.5 The Committee must keep minutes of its meetings and proceedings and keep safe all records relating to the Association.

7.6 The Committee may make rules to govern its own proceedings and the proceedings of sub-committees so long as they are not inconsistent with the provisions of this Constitution.

8. EXECUTIVE COMMITTEE: NOMINATIONS

8.1 Every candidate for election to the Committee must be nominated and seconded in writing by members of the Association and must give his or her written consent to stand for election.

8.2 Nominations and consents must be sent to the Committee within [seven] days of the notice calling the Annual General Meeting.

8.3 No person who has been an elected member of the Committee for three consecutive years is eligible for re-election for the immediately following year but may (if duly qualified) stand again for election at the Annual General Meeting in the subsequent year.

9. FINANCE

9.1 All funds belonging to or raised for the Association must be used in furthering the Objects.

9.2 No member of the Committee may be employed by the Association or receive any payment or other benefit from its funds except for reasonable out of pocket expenses properly incurred for the purposes of the Association.

9.3 The Committee is responsible for the keeping of books of accounts and for the preparation of an annual report and annual statements of account for the Association, copies of which must be sent to the Charity Commissioners as required by law.

9.4 The Committee is also responsible for arranging for the accounts of the Association to be audited by a registered auditor or, so long as the income or expenditure for the year in question does not exceed £100,000, examined by an independent examiner.

9.5 The Committee shall maintain one or more accounts for the Association at a bank or building society and make regulations governing the signatories (of whom there must be at least two) on such accounts.

10. PROPERTY

If the Association acquires any land, building, investments or other property of a permanent nature the legal title to that property must be transferred to a corporate body as holding trustee (or, in the case of freehold land, vested in the Official Custodian for Charities).

11. NOTICES

11.1 Whenever notice has to be given to the members of the Association under the provisions of this Constitution it must be delivered either by hand or by first class post to the member's last known address in the UK [or published in the Association's newsletter].

11.2 Whenever any notice is required to be given to the Committee it must be delivered by hand or sent by post to. . . .

11.3 Whenever any notice is given by post it is deemed to have been received 48 hours after posting.

12. AMENDMENT OF CONSTITUTION

The provisions of this Constitution may be amended at a General Meeting by resolution passed by [two thirds of] the members present and voting but

12.1 Notice of the terms of the proposed amendment must be given with the notice calling the meeting;

12.2 No amendment will be valid if it would [alter] [bring about a fundamental change in] the Objects;

12.3 No amendment will be valid if its effect would be that the Association ceased to be a charity according to English Law.

13. DISSOLUTION

13.1 The Association may be dissolved at a General Meeting by resolution passed by [two thirds of] the members present and voting.

13.2   In the event of a dissolution, the members of the Committee holding office will remain responsible for the orderly winding up of the affairs of the Association.

13.3   After paying or making provision for all debts and liabilities of the Association the Committee shall transfer any remaining assets to one or more registered charities having objects similar to the Objects chosen either by the members in General Meeting at the time of dissolution or afterwards by the Committee.

13.4   The Committee shall send a final statement of account to the Charity Commissioners.

14.   DISPUTES

Any dispute as to the interpretation of this Constitution or as to the propriety of any action taken or proposed by one or more members of the Committee may be resolved by unanimous decision of the Committee or referred to an independent adviser or mediator.

THIS CONSTITUTION WAS ADOPTED AT A [PUBLIC] MEETING HELD AT . . .
ON . . .

Signed
Chairman of Meeting
Secretary of Meeting

3. Memorandum and Articles of Association of a Charitable Company
[short version]

THE COMPANIES ACTS 1985 TO 1989

COMPANY LIMITED BY GUARANTEE
AND NOT HAVING A SHARE CAPITAL

MEMORANDUM OF ASSOCIATION OF [NAME]

1 Name

The name of the company ("the Trust") is . . . . . .

2 Registered Office

The registered office of the Trust will be in England or Wales.

3 Object

The Object of the Trust is to . . . . ("the Object").

In furthering the Object but not otherwise the Trust may –

(a) Organise or promote the pooling of ideas and co-operation of experts.

(b) Provide or promote lectures, discussions, classes, conferences, seminars, workshops and field visits.

(c) Publish or promote books, articles, leaflets, journals, films, broadcasts, recordings and computer programs.

(d)   Carry out or promote research on terms that the useful results are disseminated.

(e)   Train schoolchildren, students, young unemployed persons and members of the public in practical methods of . . . . .

(f)   Advise members of the public on . . . . .

(g)   Co-operate with statutory or voluntary organisations having similar aims.

(h)   Buy or lease land and buildings for use for . . . . .

(i)   Sell or let land and buildings (subject to any consents required by law).

(j)   Invest funds in any lawful manner [consistent with the Object].

(k)   Borrow money on the security of property belonging to the Trust (subject to any consents required by law).

(l)   Raise money by any lawful means excluding permanent trading.

(m) Employ paid or unpaid staff, helpers and advisers.

(n)   Support, set up, manage or assist in the support, setting up or management of other charities for similar purposes.

(o)   Take any other lawful action which is necessary or incidental to the fulfilment of the Object.

PROVIDED THAT —

(i)   The Object does not extend to the regulation of relations between workers and employers or organisations of workers and organisations of employers.

(ii) In relation to any property held by the Trust as trustee the Trust must deal with that property in accordance with the law relating to trusts.

(iii) In relation to any property held by the Trust which is subject to the jurisdiction of the Charity Commissioners for England and Wales, the Council of Management is accountable for all dealings with that property and liable for its administration and subject to the control or supervision of the Charity Commissioners and the Chancery Division of the High Court as though the members of the Council of Management were trustees of it and the Trust were not incorporated.

4 Application of Income and Property

The income and property of the Trust, whatever its source, must be used or applied only for promoting the Object; it must not be paid or transferred directly or indirectly in the form of a dividend or otherwise to the members of the Trust

PROVIDED THAT —

(i) Reasonable and proper renumeration may be paid to any officer or servant of the Trust who is not a member of the Council of Management.

(ii) Reasonable out of pocket espenses may be repaid to anyone, including a member of the Council of Management, who incurs them for the purposes of the Trust.

(iii) Interest at a reasonable rate may be paid to anyone, including a member of the Council of Management, who lends money to the Trust.

(iv) Reasonable rents or hiring fees may be paid to anyone, including a member of the Council of Management, who lets or hires land or buildings to the Trust.

(v) Where a member holds a maximum of a one hundredth share in the capital of a company a payment by the Trust to that company does not count as a benefit to the member concerned.

5 Limited Liability

The liability of members is limited.

6 **Guarantee**

Every member undertakes to pay towards the assets of the Trust a sum of not more than £10 if the Trust is wound up while he or she is a member or within a year afterwards.

7 **Distribution of Surplus**

If the Trust is wound up and after all its liabilities have been met there are any surplus assets they must not be given to the members personally but transferred to one or more other charities chosen by the members which have similar objects and preclude any benefit to their members to at least the same extent as the Trust or (if no such choice is made before the winding up) applied for some similar charitable purpose.

WE the subscribers to this Memorandum of Association wish to be formed into a Company pursuant to this Memorandum.

NAMES AND ADDRESSES OF SUBSCRIBERS

[Insert full names and addresses of first members (at least two)]

DATED

WITNESS to the above Signatures

[Insert name, address and occupation of witness]

THE COMPANIES ACTS 1985 TO 1989

COMPANY LIMITED BY GUARANTEE
AND NOT HAVING A SHARE CAPITAL

ARTICLES OF ASSOCIATION OF [NAME]

General

    1.1   In these Articles unless the contrary is indicated the following terms have the following meanings:

The Act means the Companies Act 1985 as amended by the Companies Act 1989 or any re-enactment or statutory modification of those Acts.

These Articles means these Articles of Association.

The Trust means the above named company, [Name].

The Object means the object declared in the Memorandum of Association of the Trust (see clause 3).

The Council means the Council of Management of the Trust (see article 20).

The Office means the registered office of the Trust.

The Seal means the common seal of the Trust.

Month means a calendar month.

Year means a calendar year.

Written or **in writing** means produced by any method of representing or reproducing words in permanent form.

    1.2   In these Articles unless the contrary is indicated words denoting the singular include the plural and vice versa, and words denoting the masculine include the feminine.

1.3   Otherwise any words defined in the Act or in any statutory modification of the Act have the same meaning in these Articles.

2   The number of members with which the Trust proposes to be registered is [3] but the Council may from time to time register an increase of members.

3   The Trust must observe sections 352 and 353 of the Act concerning the register of members and every member of the Trust must either sign a written consent to become a member or sign the register of members on joining.

4   The Trust is established for the Object.

5   The members of the Trust are the subscribers to the Memorandum of Association and any others whom the Council admits to membership under these Articles (see article 6).

Members

6   The members of the Trust are

(a)   the subscribers to the Memorandum of Association before registration of the Trust as a company;

(b)   other individuals in sympathy with the Object who are admitted as members by the Council in accordance with regulations made by the Council (see article 32).

7   Any member may resign his membership by written notice to the Trust and his name will be removed with immediate effect from the register of members.

8 Membership is not transferable and ceases on death.

9 A member who fails to observe these Articles may be expelled from membership by an Extraordinary meeting of the members but must be given an opportunity to state his case in person or in writing before the decision is made.

General Meetings

10 An Annual General Meeting must be held in every year on a date not more than 15 months after the last Annual General Meeting and at a time and place chosen by the Council. The first Annual General Meeting may be held at any time within 18 months of the registration of the Trust as a company.

11 All other General Meetings are called Extraordinary General Meetings.

12 The Council may convene an Extraordinary General Meeting at any time and the Secretary must do so within 21 days of receiving the requisition of at least 10 per cent of the members (see section 367 of the Act).

13 21 days' written notice to all members is required for any General Meeting, and notice must be given of any special matter to be discussed or decided (see sections 369 and 378 of the Act)

PROVIDED THAT the accidental failure to give proper notice or the non-receipt of notice by anyone entitled to receive it will not invalidate any proceeding at the meeting.

Proceedings at General Meetings

14 The functions of the Annual General Meeting are to receive the accounts and balance sheet of the Trust, to elect members of the

Council, to elect an auditor and to discuss or decide any special matter.

15   A quorum at a General Meeting is two members present in person.

16   The Chairman will normally preside at all General Meetings of the Trust. In the absence of the Chairman the members present will choose one of themselves to take the chair at that meeting.

17   The Chairman may adjourn any meeting with the consent of the members present, and no notice need be given of the time and place of the adjourned meeting unless it is to be held more than 28 days later.

18   Any matter put to the vote at a General Meeting will be decided by a simple majority on a show of hands. Every member has one vote but in the case of an equal number of votes the chairman of the meeting has a casting vote.

19   A written resolution signed by all the members has the same effect as a resolution actually passed at a General Meeting.

Council of Management

20   The work and activities of the Trust will be managed and controlled by the Council. The number of members of the Council will be [at least 3 and not more than 5].

21   The members of the Council are

       (a)   the subscribers to the Memorandum of Association and

       (b)   any other member of the Trust who is elected by the Trust in General Meeting

PROVIDED THAT no-one who is an employee or adviser paid at the expense of the Trust is eligible to stand for membership of the Council.

Proceedings of Council

22 The Council has power to regulate its own proceedings and determine the quorum for its meetings but in the absence of a determination by the Council the quorum is two members present in person, every matter is decided by majority vote and in the case of an equal number of votes the Chairman has a casting vote.

23 Any member of the Council may, and the Secretary on the request of any member of the Council must, convene a meeting of the Council by notice to each member who is in the United Kingdom.

24 The Council will from time to time elect a Chairman from among themselves and the Chairman will preside at all meetings of the Council at which he is present.

25 A quorate meeting of the Council is competent to exercise all the powers belonging to the Trust.

26 The Council may delegate any of its functions to Committees consisting of at least two members of the Council and may authorise Committees to invite other persons to attend their meetings in a non-voting capacity. All acts and proceedings of Committees must be reported promptly to the Council.

27 The Council is responsible for the keeping of proper records of meetings and resolutions of the Trust which, when signed by the Chairman, are to be taken as accurate.

28 A resolution signed by all members of the Council has the same effect as a resolution actually passed at a meeting of the Council.

29   Accidental defects in appointments or procedures do not invalidate the decisions taken.

Powers of Council

30   The Council has power to do anything in the name and on behalf of the Trust which is not reserved by these Articles to the members in General Meeting.

31   Whenever the number of members of the Council falls below three the Council may appoint another member to fill the vacancy or call a General Meeting of the Trust but may not transact any other business.

32   The Council may from time to time make and alter regulations to govern any matter not specifically covered by these Articles

PROVIDED THAT all regulations must be consistent with these Articles, with the Memorandum of Association and with the requirements of the law.

Membership of Council

33   Every member of the Council will be elected for a term ending immediately after the next Annual General Meeting of the Trust.

34   A member of the Council will immediately cease to be such a member in the following circumstances:

(a)   he becomes bankrupt or makes a composition with his creditors;

(b)   he becomes mentally or physically incapable of acting;

(c)   he is convicted of a criminal offence involving [violence or] dishonesty;

(d)   he gives written notice of his wish to resign and there remain at least two members of the Council ready and able to continue as members;

(e)   he attains the age of [70] years;

35   A member of the Council who has some personal interest in a matter to be decided by the Council must declare his interest, absent himself from the discussion and refrain from voting on the matter.

The Secretary

36   The Council will appoint (and may remove) either one of themselves (without payment) or some other fit person (who may be remunerated) as Secretary of the Trust.

The Seal

37   The Seal may only be used with the authority of the Council and in the presence of either two members of the Council or one member of the Council and the Secretary. Any person dealing with the Trust in good faith and any purchaser may assume that the seal if witnessed in this way has been properly used.

Application of Funds

38   The income and property of the Trust may only be held, used or applied in fulfilment of the Object as the Council from time to time directs.

Accounts

39   The Council is responsible for the keeping of accounting records as required by the Act (see section 221).

40   The books of account must be kept at the Office and copies must be sent to the members and others entitled to copies and to the Charity Commissioners for England and Wales (see section 238 of the Act and section 45 of the Charities Act 1993).

41   At the Annual General Meeting the Council must present an income
      and expenditure account for the period since the previous account
      until a date within the last six months, and a balance sheet made up to
      the end of the same period. The accounts must be accompanied by
      reports from the Auditor and the Council. A copy of the accounts with
      the Auditor's report must be sent to the Auditor and to every member
      at least 21 days in advance of the Annual General Meeting at which
      they are to be presented.

Audit

42   The Auditor must be appointed in the manner required by the Act (see
      sections 235 to 237).

Notices

43   The Trust may serve a notice on a member either personally or
      through the post to his registered address in the United Kingdom.

44   Notices served by post are taken to have been received three days
      after posting.

Dissolution

45   Clause 8 of the Memorandum of Association relating to the winding up
      of the Trust has effect as though it were repeated here.

NAMES AND ADDRESSES OF SUBSCRIBERS

[As for subscribers to memorandum]

DATED

WITNESS to the above Signatures

[As before]

4. Memorandum and Articles of Association

[Jordans Recommended Forms (long version)]

THE COMPANIES ACTS 1985 TO 1989

COMPANY LIMITED BY GUARANTEE
AND NOT HAVING A SHARE CAPITAL

MEMORANDUM OF ASSOCIATION OF
[NAME]

1. The Company's name is [NAME].

2. The Company's registered office is to be situated in England and Wales.

3. The Company's objects are:-

[Insert here brief and specific main objects, which must be within the four legal heads of charity –

the relief of poverty/the advancement of education/the advancement of religion/other purposes beneficial to the community.]

In furtherance of the above objects but not further or otherwise the Company shall have the following powers:-

[Insert here supporting powers specific to the Company's objects eg:-

(a)   To offer an information and advice service to voluntary groups and community organisations and to those suffering from mobility problems in the area of ....;

(b)   To promote research, experimental work, scientific investigation and development;

(c)   To co-ordinate facilities and services offered by statutory and official bodies, charities and the voluntary sector for the benefit of the disabled;

(d)   To publish surveys, leaflets, books, and information on matters of concern to those with mobility problems and those engaged in promoting their welfare and interests;

etc.]

[continue consecutive lettering of these sub-clauses:-]

() Subject to such consents as may be required by law, to borrow and raise money for the furtherance of the objects of the Company in such manner and on such security as the Company may think fit.

() To raise funds and to invite and receive contributions from any person or persons whatsoever by way of subscription, donation or otherwise provided that this shall be without prejudice to the ability of the Company to disclaim any gift, legacy or bequest in whole or in part in such circumstances as the Company may think fit and provided also that the Company shall not undertake any permanent trading activities in raising funds for the above mentioned charitable objects.

() To lend money and give credit to, to take security for such loans or credit from, and to guarantee and become or give security for the performance of contracts and obligations by, any person or company.

() To draw, make, accept, endorse, discount, execute and issue promissory notes, bills of exchange, bills of lading, warrants, and other negotiable, transferable, or mercantile instruments.

() To subscribe for either absolutely or conditionally or otherwise acquire and hold shares, stocks, debentures, debenture stock or other securities or obligations of any other company.

() To invest the moneys of the Company not immediately required for the furtherance of its objects in or upon such investments, securities or property as may be thought fit, subject nevertheless to such conditions (if any) and such consents (if any) as may for the time being be imposed or required by law.

() To purchase, take on lease or in exchange, hire or otherwise acquire any real or personal property and any rights or privileges and to construct, maintain and alter any buildings or erections which the Company may think necessary for the promotion of its objects.

() Subject to such consents as may be required by law, to sell, let, mortgage, dispose of or turn to account all or any of the property or assets of the Company with a view to the furtherance of its objects.

() Subject to Clause 4 hereof to employ and pay such architects, surveyors, solicitors and other professional persons, workmen, clerks and other staff as are necessary for the furtherance of the objects of the Company.

() To make all reasonable and necessary provision for the payment of pensions and superannuation to or on behalf of employees and their widows and other dependants.

() To make payments towards insurance for any Director, officer or Auditor against personal liability for acts properly undertaken by them or undertaken by them in breach of trust but under an honest mistake.

() To subscribe to, become a member of, or amalgamate or co-operate with any other charitable organisation, institution, society or body not formed or established for purposes of profit (whether incorporated or not and whether in Great Britain or Northern Ireland or elsewhere) whose objects are wholly or in part similar to those of the Company and which by its constitution prohibits the distribution of its income and property amongst its members to an extent at least as great as is imposed on the Company under or by virtue of Clause 4 hereof and to purchase or otherwise acquire and undertake all such part of the property, assets, liabilities and engagements as may lawfully be acquired or undertaken by the Company of any such charitable organisation, institution, society or body.

() To establish and support or aid the establishment and support of any charitable trusts, associations or institutions and to subscribe or guarantee money for charitable purposes in any way connected with or calculated to further any of the objects of the Company.

() To do all or any of the things hereinbefore authorised either alone or in conjunction with any other charitable organisation, institution, society or body with which this Company is authorised to amalgamate.

() To pay all or any expenses incurred in connection with the promotion, formation and incorporation of the Company.

() To do all such other lawful things as are necessary for the attainment of the above objects or any of them.

Provided that:-

(a)   In case the Company shall take or hold any property which may be subject to any trusts, the Company shall only deal with or invest the same in such manner as allowed by law, having regard to such trusts.

(b)   The objects of the Company shall not extend to the regulation of relations between workers and employers or organisations of workers and organisations of employers.

(c)   In case the Company shall take or hold any property subject to the jurisdiction of the Charity Commissioners for England and Wales, the Company shall not sell, mortgage, charge or lease the same without such authority, approval or consent as may be required by law, and as regards any such property the Council of Management or Governing Body of the Company shall be chargeable for any such property that may come into their hands and shall be answerable and accountable for their own acts receipts neglects and defaults, and for the due administration of such property in the same manner and to the same extent as they would as such Council of Management or Governing Body have been if no incorporation had been effected, and the incorporation of the Company shall not diminish or impair any control or authority exercisable by the Chancery Division of the Charity Commissioners over such Council of Management or Governing Body but they shall as regards any such property be subject jointly and separately to such control or authority as if the Company were not incorporated.

4.   The income and property of the Company shall be applied solely towards the promotion of its objects as set forth in this Memorandum of Association and no portion thereof shall be paid or transferred, directly or indirectly, by way of dividend, bonus or otherwise howsoever by way of profit, to members of the Company, and no member of its Council of Management or Governing Body shall be appointed to any office of the Company paid by salary or fees or receive any remuneration or other benefit in money or money's worth from the Company.

Provided that nothing herein shall prevent any payment in good faith by the Company:-

(a)   of reasonable and proper remuneration to any member, officer or servant of the Company (not being a member of its Council of

Management or Governing Body) for any services rendered to the Company;

(b)   of interest on money lent by any member of the Company or of its Council of Management or Governing Body at a reasonable and proper rate per annum for exceeding 2 per cent less than the published base lending rate of a clearing bank to be selected by the Council of Management or Governing Body;

(c)   of reasonable and proper rent for premises demised or let by any member of the Company or of its Council of Management or Governing Body;

(d)   of fees, remuneration or other benefit in money or money's worth to any company of which a member of the Council of Management or Governing Body may also be a member holding not more than 1/100 part of the capital of that company; and

(e)   to any member of its Council of Management or Governing Body of reasonable out-of-pocket expenses.

5.   The liability of the members is limited.

6.   Every member of the Company undertakes to contribute such amount as may be required (not exceeding £1) to the Company's assets if it should be wound up while he is a member, or within one year after he ceases to be a member, for payment of the Company's debts and liabilities contracted before he ceases to be a member, and of the costs, charges and expenses of winding up, and for the adjustment of the rights of the contributories among themselves.

7.   If upon the winding-up or dissolution of the Company there remains, after the satisfaction of all its debts and liabilities, any property whatsoever, the same shall not be paid to or distributed among the members of the Company, but shall be given or transferred to some other charitable institution or institutions having objects similar to the objects of the Company, and which shall prohibit the distribution of its or their income and property to an extent at least as great as is imposed on the Company under or by virtue of Clause 4 hereof, such institution or institutions to be determined by the members of the Company at or before the time of dissolution, and if and so far as effect cannot be given to such provision, then to some other charitable object.

THE COMPANIES ACTS 1985 TO 1989

COMPANY LIMITED BY GUARANTEE
AND NOT HAVING A SHARE CAPITAL

ARTICLES OF ASSOCIATION OF

INTERPRETATION

1.   In these Articles:-

"the Act" means the Companies Act 1985, but so that any reference to any provision of the Act shall be deemed to include a reference to any statutory modification or re-enactment of that provision for the time being in force.

"the Council" means the Council of Management of the Company.

"the seal" means the common seal of the Company.

"secretary" means any person appointed to perform the duties of the secretary of the Company.

"the United Kingdom" means Great Britain and Northern Ireland.

Expressions referring to writing shall, unless the contrary intention appears, be construed as including references to printing, lithography, photography, and other modes of representing or reproducing words in a visible form.

Unless the context otherwise requires, words or expressions contained in these Articles shall bear the same meaning as in the Act or any statutory modification or re-eneactment thereof for the time being in force.

OBJECTS

2.   The Company is established for the objects expressed in the Memorandum of Association.

MEMBERS

3.   The subscribers to the Memorandum of Association and such other persons as the Council shall admit to membership shall be members of the Company. Every member of the Company shall either sign a written consent to become a member or sign the register of members on becoming a member.

4.   Unless the members of the Council or the Company in General Meeting shall make other provision pursuant to the powers contained in Article 66, the members of the Council may in their absolute discretion permit any member of the Company to retire, provided (regardless of any other provision pursuant to Article 66) that after such retirement the number of members is not less than three.

GENERAL MEETINGS

5.   The Company shall in each year hold a General Meeting as its Annual General Meeting in addition to any other meetings in that year, and shall specify the meeting as such in the notices calling it; and not more than fifteen months shall elapse between the date of one Annual General Meeting of the Company and that of the next. Provided that so long as the Company holds its first Annual General Meeting within eighteen months of its incorporation, it need not hold it in the year of its incorporation or in the following year. The Annual General Meeting shall be held at such time and place as the Council shall appoint. All General Meetings other than Annual General Meetings shall be called Extraordinary General Meetings.

6.   The Council may, whenever they think fit, convene an Extraordinary General Meeting, and Extraordinary General Meetings shall also be convened on such requisition, or, in default, may be convened by such requisitionists, as provided by Section 368 of the Act. If at any time there are not within the United Kingdom sufficient members of the Council capable of acting to form a quorum, any member of the Council or any two members of the Company may convene an Extraordinary General Meeting in the same manner as nearly as possible as that in which meetings may be convened by the Council.

NOTICE OF GENERAL MEETINGS

7.   An Annual General Meeting and a meeting called for the passing of a special resolution shall be called by twenty-one days' notice in writing at

the least, and a meeting of the Company other than an Annual General Meeting or a meeting for the passing of a special resolution shall be called by fourteen days' notice in writing at the least. The notice shall be exclusive of the day on which it is served or deemed to be served and of the day for which it is given, and shall specify the place, the day and the hour of meeting and, in case of special business, the general nature of that business and shall be given, in manner hereinafter mentioned or in such other manner, in any, as may be prescribed by the Company in general meeting, to such persons as are, under the Articles of the Company, entitled to receive such notices from the Company:

Provided that a meeting of the Company shall, notwithstanding that it is called by shorter notice than that specified in this Article, be deemed to have been duly called if it is so agreed:-

(a) in the case of a meeting called as the Annual General Meeting, by all the members entitled to attend and vote thereat; and

(b) in the case of any other meeting, by a majority in number of the members having a right to attend and vote at the meeting, being a majority together representing (subject to the provisions of any elective resolution of the Company for the time being in force) not less than ninety-five per cent of the total voting rights at that meeting of all the members.

8.   The accidental omission to give notice of a meeting to, or the non-receipt of notice of a meeting by, any person entitled to receive notice shall not invalidate the proceedings at that meeting.

PROCEEDINGS AT GENERAL MEETINGS

9.   No business shall be transacted at any General Meeting unless a quorum of members is present at the time when the meeting proceeds to business; save as herein otherwise provided, three members present in person or one-tenth of the membership, whichever shall be the greater shall be a quorum. If within half an hour from the time appointed for the meeting a quorum is not present, the meeting, if convened upon the requisition of members, shall be dissolved; in any other case it shall stand adjourned to the same day in the next week, at the same time and place, or to such other day and at such other time and place as the Council may determine.

10.   The chairman, if any, of the Council shall preside as chairman at every General Meeting of the Company, or if there is no such chairman, or if

he shall not be present within fifteen minutes after the time appointed for the holding of the meeting or is unwilling to act the members of the Council present shall elect one of their number to be chairman of the meeting.

11.   If at any meeting no member of the Council is willing to act as chairman or if no member of the Council is present within fifteen minutes after the time appointed for holding the meeting, the members present shall choose one of their number to be chairman of the meeting.

12.   The chairman may, with the consent of any meeting at which a quorum is present (and shall if so directed by the meeting), adjourn the meeting from time to time and from place to place, but no business shall be transacted at any adjourned meeting other than the business left un-finished at the meeting from which the adjournment took place. When a meeting is adjourned for thirty days or more, notice of the adjourned meeting shall be given as in the case of an original meeting. Save as aforesaid it shall not be necessary to give any notice of an adjournment or of the business to be transacted at an adjourned meeting.

13.   At any General Meeting a resolution put to the vote of the meeting shall be decided on a show of hands unless a poll is (before or on the declaration of the result of the show of hands) demanded:-

(a)   by the chairman; or

(b)   by at least two members present in person or by proxy; or

(c)   by any member or members present in person or by proxy and representing not less than one-tenth of the total voting rights of all the members having the right to vote at the meeting.

Unless a poll be so demanded a declaration by the chairman that a resolution has on a show of hands been carried or carried unanimously, or by a particular majority, or lost and an entry to that effect in the book containing the minutes of proceedings of the Company shall be conclusive evidence of the fact without proof of the number or proportion of the votes recorded in favour of or against such resolution.

The demand for a poll may be withdrawn.

14.   Except as provided in Article 16, if a poll is duly demanded it shall be taken in such manner as the chairman directs, and the result of the poll

shall be deemed to be the resolution of the meeting at which the poll was demanded.

15.   In the case of an equality of votes, whether on a show of hands or on a poll, the chairman of the meeting at which the show of hands takes place or at which the poll is demanded, shall be entitled to a second or casting vote.

16.   A poll demanded on the election of a chairman, or on a question of adjournment, shall be taken forthwith. A poll demanded on any other question shall be taken at such time as the chairman of the meeting directs, and any business other than that upon which a poll has been demanded may be proceeded with pending the taking of the poll.

VOTES OF MEMBERS

17.   Every member shall have one vote.

18.   A member of unsound mind, or in respect of whom an order has been made by any court having jurisdiction in lunacy, may vote, whether on a show of hands or on a poll, by his committee, receiver, curator bonis or other person in the nature of a committee, receiver, or curator bonis appointed by that court, and any such committee, receiver, curator bonis or other person may, on a poll, vote by proxy.

19.   No member shall be entitled to vote at any General Meeting unless all moneys presently payable by him to the Company have been paid.

20.   (a)   Any member of the Company entitled to attend and vote at a General Meeting shall be entitled to appoint another person (whether a member or not) as his proxy to attend and vote instead of him and any proxy so appointed shall have the same right as the member to speak at the Meeting.

        (b)   On a poll votes may be given either personally or by proxy.

21.   The instrument appointing a proxy shall be in writing under the hand of the appointor or of his attorney duly authorised in writing, or, if the appointor is a corporation, either under seal or under the hand of an officer or attorney duly authorised. A proxy need not be a member of the Company.

22.   The instrument appointing a proxy and the power of attorney or other authority, if any, under which it is signed or a notarially certified copy of that power or authority shall be deposited at the registered office of the Company or at such other place within the United Kingdom as is specified for that purpose in the notice convening the meeting, not less than 48 hours before the time for holding the meeting or adjourned meeting at which the person named in the instrument proposes to vote, or, in the case of a poll, not less than 24 hours before the time appointed for the taking of the poll, and in default the instrument of proxy shall not be treated as valid.

23.   An instrument appointing a proxy shall be in the following form or a form as near thereto as circumstances admit:-

"   Limited.
I/We   of   in the County of   being a member/members of the above named Company, hereby appoint   of   or failing him   of   as my/our proxy to vote for me/us on my/our behalf at the (Annual or Extraordinary, as the case may be) General Meeting of the Company to be held on the   day of   19 , and at any adjournment thereof.

Signed this   day of   19 ."

24.   Where it is desired to afford members an opportunity of voting for or against a resolution the instrument appointing a proxy shall be in the following form or a form as near thereto as circumstances admit:-

"   Limited.
I/We   of   in the County of   being a member/members of the above named Company, hereby appoint   of   or failing him   of   as my/our proxy to vote for me/us on my/our behalf at the (Annual or Extraordinary, as the case may be) General Meeting of the Company to be held on the   day of   19 , and at any adjournment thereof.

Signed this   day of   19 ."

This form is to be used *in favour of the resolution.
                        against

Unless otherwise instructed, the proxy will vote as he thinks fit.

[*Strike out whichever is not desired]

25. The instrument appointing a proxy shall be deemed to confer authority to demand or join in demanding a poll.

26. A vote given in accordance with the terms of an instrument of proxy shall be valid notwithstanding the previous death or insanity of the principal or revocation of the proxy or of the authority under which the proxy was executed, provided that no intimation in writing of such death, insanity or revocation as aforesaid shall have been received by the Company at the office before the commencement of the meeting or adjourned meeting at which the proxy is used.

CORPORATIONS ACTING BY REPRESENTATIVES AT MEETINGS

27. Any corporation which is a member of the Company may by resolution of its Council or other governing body authorise such person as it thinks fit to act as its representative at any meeting of the Company, and the person so authorised shall be entitled to exercise the same powers on behalf of the corporation which he represents as that corporation could exercise if it were an individual member of the Company.

COUNCIL OF MANAGEMENT

28. The maximum number of the members of the Council shall be determined by the Company in General Meeting, but unless and until so fixed there shall be no maximum number and the minimum number of members of the Council shall be three.

29. The members of the Council shall be paid all reasonable out of pocket, hotel and other expenses properly incurred by them in attending and returning from meetings of the Council or any committee of the Council or General Meetings of the Company or in connection with the business of the Company.

BORROWING POWERS

30. The Council may in furtherance of the objects of the Company but not otherwise exercise all the powers of the Company to borrow money, and, subject always to Sections 38 and 39 of the Charities Act 1993, to

mortgage or charge its undertaking and property, or any part thereof, and to issue debentures, debenture stock and other securities, whether outright or as security for any debt, liability or obligation of the Company or of any third party subject to such consents as may be required by law.

POWERS AND DUTIES OF THE COUNCIL

31.   (a)   The business of the Company shall be managed by the Council, who may pay all expenses incurred in promoting and registering the Company, and may exercise all such powers of the Company as are not, by the Act or by these Articles, required to be exercised by the Company in General Meeting, subject nevertheless to the provisions of the Act or these Articles and to such regulations, being not inconsistent with the aforesaid provisions, as may be prescribed by the Company in General Meeting; but no regulation made by the Company in General Meeting shall invalidate any prior act of the Council which would have been valid if that regulation had not been made.

         (b)   In the exercise of the aforesaid powers and in the management of the business of the Company, the members of the Council shall always be mindful that they are charity trustees within the definition of Section 97 of the Charities Act 1993 as the persons having the general control and management of the administration of a charity.

32.   All cheques, promissory notes, drafts, bills of exchange and other negotiable instruments, and all receipts for moneys paid to the Company, shall be signed, drawn, accepted, endorsed or otherwise executed, as the case may be, in such manner as the Council shall from time to time by resolution determine.

33.   The Council shall cause minutes to be made in books provided for the purpose:-

         (a)   of all appointments of officers made by the Council;

         (b)   of the names of the members of the Council present at each meeting of the Council and of any committee of the Council;

         (c)   of all resolutions and proceedings at all meetings of the Company, and of the Council and of committees of the Council.

DISQUALIFICATION OF MEMBERS OF THE COUNCIL

34.   The office of member of the Council shall be vacated if the member:-

(a) becomes bankrupt or makes any arrangement or composition with his creditors generally; or

(b) becomes prohibited from being a member of the Council by reason of Section 72 of the Charities Act 1993 or any order made under any provision of the Act or any other statute or otherwise becomes prohibited by law from being a member of the Council; or

(c) becomes incapable by reason of mental disorder, illness or injury of managing and administering his property and affairs; or

(d) resigns his office by notice in writing to the Company; or

(e) is directly or indirectly interested in any contract with the Company and fails to declare the nature of his interest in manner required by Section 317 of the Act.

35. A member of the Council shall not vote in respect of any contract in which he is interested or any matter arising thereout, and if he does so vote his vote shall not be counted.

ROTATION OF MEMBERS OF THE COUNCIL

36. At the first Annual General Meeting of the Company all the members of the Council shall retire from office, and at the Annual General Meeting in every subsequent year one-third of the members of the Council for the time being or, if their number is not three or a multiple of three, then the number nearest one-third, shall retire from office.

37. The members of the Council to retire in every year shall be those who have been longest in office since their last election, but as between persons who became members of the Council on the same day those to retire shall (unless they otherwise agree among themselves) be determined by lot.

38. A retiring member of the Council shall be eligible for re-election.

39. The Company at the meeting at which a member of the Council retires in manner aforesaid may fill the vacated office by electing a person thereto, and in default the retiring member of the Council shall, if offering himself for re-election, be deemed to have been re-elected, unless at such meeting it is expressly resolved not to fill such vacated office or unless a resolution for

the re-election of such member of the Council shall have been put to the meeting and lost.

40.   No person other than a member of the Council retiring at the meeting shall unless recommended by the Council be eligible for election to the office of member of the Council at any General Meeting unless, not less than three nor more than twenty-one days before the date appointed for the meeting, there shall have been left at the registered office of the Company notice in writing signed by a member duly qualified to attend and vote at the meeting for which such notice is given, of his intention to propose such person for election, and also notice in writing signed by that person of his willingness to be elected.

41.   The Company may from time to time by ordinary resolution increase or reduce the number of members of the Council, and may also determine in what rotation the increased or reduced number is to go out of office.

42.   The Council shall have power at any time, and from time to time, to appoint any person to be a member of the Council, either to fill a casual vacancy or as an addition to the existing members of the Council, but so that the total number of members of the Council shall not at any time exceed any maximum number fixed in accordance with these Articles. Any member of the Council so appointed shall hold office only until the next following Annual General Meeting, and shall then be eligible for re-election, but shall not be taken into account in determining the members of the Council who are to retire by rotation at such meeting.

43.   The Company may by ordinary resolution, of which special notice has been given in accordance with Section 379 of the Act, remove any member of the Council before the expiration of his period of office notwithstanding anything in these Articles or in any agreement between the Company and such member of the Council.

44.   The Company may by ordinary resolution appoint another person in place of a member of the Council removed from office under the immediately preceding Article. Without prejudice to the powers of the Council under Article 42 the Company in General Meeting may appoint any person to be a member of the Council either to fill a casual vacancy or as an additional member of the Council. The person appointed to till such a vacancy shall be subject to retirement at the same time as if he had become a member of the Council on the day on which the member of the Council in whose place he is appointed was last elected a member of the Council.

PROCEEDINGS OF THE COUNCIL

45.   The Council may meet together for the despatch of business, adjourn, and otherwise regulate their meetings, as they think fit. Questions arising at any meeting shall be decided by a majority of votes. In the case of an equality of votes the chairman shall have a second or casting vote. A member of the Council may, and the secretary on the requisition of a member of the Council shall, at any time summon a meeting of the Council. It shall not be necessary to give notice of a meeting of the Council to any member of the Council for the time being absent from the United Kingdom.

46.   The quorum necessary for the transaction of the business of the Council may be fixed by the Council, and unless so fixed shall be three or one-third of the number of members of the Council for the time being whichever shall be the greater number.

47.   The continuing members of the Council may act notwithstanding any vacancy in their body, but, if and so long as their number is reduced below the number fixed by or pursuant to the Articles of the Company as the necessary quorum of members of the Council, the continuing members or member of the Council may act for the purpose of increasing the number of members of the Council to that number, or of summoning a General Meeting of the Company, but for no other purpose.

48.   The Council may elect a chairman of their meetings and determine the period for which he is to hold office; but, if no such chairman is elected, or if at any meeting the chairman is not present within five minutes after the time appointed for holding the same, the members of the Council present may choose one of their number to be chairman of the meeting.

49.   The Council may delegate any of their powers to committees consisting of such majority of members of their body as they think fit; any committee so formed shall in the exercise of the powers so delegated conform to any regulations that may be imposed on it by the Council and shall fully and promptly report all acts and proceedings to the Council as soon as is reasonably practicable.

50.   A committee may elect a chairman of its meetings; if no such chairman is elected, or if at any meeting the chairman is not present within five minutes after the time appointed for holding the same, the members present may choose one of their number to be chairman of the meeting.

51.   A committee may meet and adjourn as it thinks proper. Questions arising at any meeting shall be determined by a majority of votes of the members present, and in the case of an equality of votes the chairman shall have a second or casting vote.

52.   All acts done by any meeting of the Council or of a committee of the Council, or by any person acting as a member of the Council, shall notwithstanding that it be afterwards discovered that there was some defect in the appointment of any such member of the Council or person acting as aforesaid, or that they or any of them were disqualified, be as valid as if every such person had been duly appointed and was qualified to be a member of the Council.

53.   A resolution in writing, signed by all the members of the Council for the time being entitled to receive notice of a meeting of the Council, shall be as valid and effectual as if it had been passed at a meeting of the Council duly convened and held.

SECRETARY

54.   Subject to Section 13(5) of the Act, the secretary shall be appointed by the Council for such term, at such remuneration and upon such conditions as the Council may think fit; and any secretary so appointed may be removed by it: Provided always that no member of the Council may occupy the salaried position of secretary.

55.   A provision of the Act or these Articles requiring or authorising a thing to be done by or to a member of the Council and the secretary shall not be satisfied by its being done by or to the same person acting both as member of the Council and as, or in place of, the secretary.

THE SEAL

56.   If the Company has a seal the Council shall provide for its safe custody and it shall only be used by the authority of the Council or of a committee of the Council authorised by the Council in that behalf, and every instrument to which the seal shall be affixed shall be signed by a member of the Council and shall be countersigned by the secretary or by a second member of the Council or by some other person appointed by the Council for the purpose.

ACCOUNTS

57.   The Council shall cause accounting records to be kept in accordance with the provisions of the Act.

58.   The accounting records shall be kept at the registered office of the Company or, subject to the provisions of the Act, at such other place or places as the Council thinks fit, and shall always be open to the inspection of the officers of the Company.

59.   The Council shall from time to time determine whether and to what extent and at what times and places and under what conditions or regulations the accounts and books of the Company or any of them shall be open to the inspection of members not being members of the Council, and no member (not being a member of the Council) shall have any right of inspecting any account or book or document of the Company except as conferred by statute or authorised by the Council or by the Company in General Meeting.

60.   The Council shall from time to time in accordance with the provisions of the Act, cause to be prepared and to be laid before the Company in General Meeting such profit and loss accounts, balance sheets, group accounts (if any) and reports as are referred to in those provisions.

61.   A copy of every balance sheet (including every document required by law to be annexed thereto) which is to be laid before the Company in General Meeting, together with a copy of the auditor's report, and Council's report, shall not less than twenty-one days before the date of the meeting be sent to every member of the Company and every person entitled to receive notice of General Meetings of the Company.

AUDIT

62.   Auditors shall be appointed and their duties regulated in accordance with the provisions of the Act.

NOTICES

63.   A notice may be given by the Company to any member either personally or by sending it by post to him or to his registered address, or (if

he has no registered address within the United Kingdom) to the address, if any, within the United Kingdom supplied by him to the Company for the giving of notice to him. Where a notice is sent by post, service of the notice shall be deemed to be effected by properly addressing, prepaying and posting a letter containing the notice, and to have been effected in the case of a notice of a meeting at the expiration of 24 hours after the letter containing the same is posted, and in any other case at the time at which the letter would be delivered in the ordinary course of post.

64. Notice of every General Meeting shall be given in any manner hereinbefore authorised to:-

(a)   every member except those members who (having no registered address within the United Kingdom) have not supplied to the Company an address within the United Kingdom for the giving of notices to them;

(b)   every person being a trustee in bankruptcy of a member where the member but for his bankruptcy would be entitled to receive notice of the meeting;

(c)   the auditors for the time being of the Company; and

(d)   each member of the Council.

No other person shall be entitled to receive notices of General Meetings.

DISSOLUTION

65.   Clause 7 of the Memorandum of Association relating to the winding up and dissolution of the Company shall have effect as if the provisions thereof were repeated in these Articles.

RULES OR BYE LAWS

66.   (a)   The Council may from time to time make such Rules or Bye Laws as it may deem necessary or expedient or convenient for the proper conduct and management of the Company and for the purposes of prescribing classes of and conditions of membership, and in particular but without prejudice to the generality of the foregoing, it may by such Rules or Bye Laws regulate:-

(i)   The admission and classification of members of the Company, and the rights and privileges of such members, and the conditions of membership and the terms on which members may resign or have their membership terminated and the entrance fees, subscriptions and other fees or payments to be made by members.

(ii)   The conduct of members of the Company in relation to one another, and to the Company's servants.

(iii)   The setting aside of the whole or any part or parts of the Company's premises at any particular time or times or for any particular purpose or purposes.

(iv)   The procedure at General Meetings and meetings of the Council and Committees of the Council in so far as such procedure is not regulated by these presents.

(v)   And, generally, all such matters as are commonly the subject matter of Company rules.

(b)   The Company in General Meeting shall have power to alter or repeal the Rules or Bye Laws and to make additions thereto and the Council shall adopt such means as they deem sufficient to bring to the notice of members of the Company all such Rules or Bye Laws, which so long as they shall be in force, shall be binding on all members of the Company. Provided, nevertheless, that no Rule or Bye Law shall be inconsistent with, or shall affect or repeal anything contained in, the Memorandum or Articles of Association of the Company.

INDEMNITY

67.   (a)   Every member of the Council or other officer or Auditor of the Company shall be indemnified out of the assets of the Company against all losses or liabilities which he may sustain or incur in or about the execution of the duties of his office or otherwise in relation thereto, including any liability incurred by him in defending any proceedings, whether civil or criminal, in which judgment is given in his favour or in which he is acquitted or in connection with any application under Section 727 of the Act in which relief is granted to him by the Court, and no member of the Council or other officer shall be liable for any loss, damage or misfortune which may happen to or be incurred by the Company in the execution of the duties of

his office or in relation thereto. But this Article shall only have effect in so far as its provisions are not avoided by Section 310 of the Act.

(b)   The members of the Council shall have power to purchase and maintain for any member of the Council, officer or Auditor of the Company insurance against personal liability for acts properly undertaken by them or undertaken by them in breach of trust but under an honest mistake.

5. Grant Agreement

THIS AGREEMENT made the . . . . . . between

(1)   [Names and addresses of trustees of grant-making charity] as trustees of the [Name of grant-making charity] ("the Trust") and

(2)   [Names and addresses of committee of recipient charity] as trustees of the [Name of recipient charity] ("the Charity")

WITNESSES AS FOLLOWS

Recitals

(1)   The Trust is established for the purpose of (Object of Trust)

(2)   In furtherance of that purpose the Trust has agreed to provide by instalments over . . . years a grant not exceeding £. . . . in total to the Charity to assist it in carrying out the project described in the Schedule below ("the Project")

Grant

The Trust undertakes to pay to the Charity and the Charity agrees to accept the following sums on the following conditions:

1.   The Trust will pay to the Charity within 10 days of this Agreement the sum of £. . . . ("the first instalment");

2.   The Charity will use the first instalment and all subsequent instalments for the sole purpose of the Project;

3.   Within [6 months] of the receipt of each instalment the Charity will report in writing to the Trust on the way in which it has been applied and on the progress of the Project;

4.   Within 6 weeks of the receipt of the report from the Charity the Trust will notify the Charity in writing of the date when the next instalment will be paid and the amount thereof;

5. The Charity will report in writing on the application of each instalment and on the progress of the Project and will also reply to any specific questions concerning the Project raised by the Trust at any time;

6. The Trust may inspect the Project at any reasonable time on giving at least 7 days' notice in writing to the Charity; and

7. The Trust is entitled to receive from the Charity a copy of its annual reports and statements of account so long as this Agreement remains in force.

Termination

1. This Agreement will come to an end in the following circumstances:

    (i)   the Charity ceases to exist or to operate or to be a registered charity;

    (ii)   a receiver and manager is appointed for the Charity;

    (iii) any trustee or officer of the charity is suspended or removed by order of the Court or the Charity Commissioners;

    (iv)   the Charity fails to comply with the terms of this Agreement;

    (v)   the Charity does not proceed with the Project or

    (vi)   The Project is completed.

2. If this Agreement is terminated the Charity will be liable to repay to the Trust all sums received from the Trust under this Agreement which have not been used for the Project [with simple interest at the rate of . . . per cent per annum calculated from the date of receipt].

3. If the Project is completed the Charity must provide a final report to the Trust not less than 12 months after the last payment.

Variation

This Agreement may be varied at any time by written agreement between the Trust and the Charity.

Contacts

The Trust will deal with the Charity under this Agreement through its [Director] and the Charity will deal with the Trust through its [Project Manager].

Disputes

In the event of any dispute over the effect of this Agreement or whether there has been a breach of its terms the Trust and the Charity may refer the question to the Charity Commissioners for their opinion or advice or may jointly appoint a mediator to assist in resolving the matter.

Execution

This Agreement is executed on behalf of the Trust by two of the trustees thereof authorised by resolution under section 82 of the Charities Act 1993 and on behalf of the Charity by two of the members of its committee of management authorised by resolution under the same provision.

SCHEDULE

[Full description of project]

Signatures

6.   Fundraising Agreement

THIS AGREEMENT made the [date] BETWEEN

(1)   [Name & address of Charity or of trustee body if incorporated]
[Full names & addresses of Charity Trustees if unincorporated]
("the Charity")

and

(2)   [Name & address of fundraiser] ("the Fundraiser")

WITNESSES as follows:

1.   INTRODUCTION

   1.1   The Charity is a [registered] charity established for [summary of
         objects of Charity]

   1.2   The Charity desires to raise or collect funds in order to support
         [that purpose] [more specific project for which funds are to be
         raised] ("the Project") [and has selected a target of £. . . .]

   1.3   The Charity has authorised the Fundraiser to raise or collect
         funds on behalf of the Charity for the Project in accordance with
         the terms of this agreement

2.   METHOD OF FUNDRAISING

   2.1   The Fundraiser will observe all rules of laws, bye-laws and
         regulations relevant to the fundraising methods used

   2.2   The methods of fundraising to be used will be [specify methods
         chosen. eg direct mail, concerts or other events, lotteries etc.].
         The Fundraiser must obtain the prior written approval of the
         Charity of the use of any other methods for raising or collecting
         funds

   2.3   The copyright in all literature and art-work designed or produced
         by or on behalf of the Fundraiser in relation to the Project will
         belong to the Charity and must be marked as such

2.4 All funds raised or collected for the Project must be paid into the Charity's Bank Account at [Bank and branch], account no. . . . , not less than [4] weeks after receipt

2.5 All gifts in kind received by the Fundraiser, and the originals of all executed covenants, gift aid certificates and other documentary evidence of gifts (or promises of gifts), in connection with the Project must be handed over to the Charity within [7] days of receipt

2.6 The Fundraiser must treat as confidential all information concerning the Charity which [he][she][it] acquires in consequence of or in connection with this Agreement or the Project

2.7 The Fundraiser must keep proper records of all receipts and outgoings relating to the Project

2.8 The Fundraiser must allow the Charity at any time during office hours on not less than 24 hours' notice to the Fundraiser to inspect all or any of the records or other items held by the Fundraiser, including records kept in computerised form, which relate to the Project

3. MEETINGS AND REPORTS

3.1 The Fundraiser and the [fund-raising committee of] the Charity will hold regular [bi-monthly] meetings (to be held at the offices of the Charity at [address]). The purpose of such meetings will be for the Fundraiser to report progress on the Project and discuss future plans, and for the [Charity][committee] to review the working of this Agreement

3.2 In addition to attending such meetings the Fundraiser will provide to the Charity a written progress report on the Project every [three] months while this Agreement is in force

3.3 Either party may by written notice to the other require the holding of a special meeting to discuss any matter of urgency or exceptional importance relating to the Project or to the working of this Agreement

4. PERIOD OF AGREEMENT

    4.1   This Agreement will expire on [date] unless terminated earlier under clause 5 below

    4.2   The Fundraiser must provide a final written report to the Charity on or before the date of expiry

    4.3   On expiry, this Agreement may be extended by written agreement between the Charity and the Fundraiser for a further period [not exceeding . . months] to be specified in writing

5. TERMINATION

    5.1   This Agreement will come to an end in the following circumstances:

          (i)   Achievement or substantial achievement of the Project

          (ii)   On the expiry of [6 weeks] after notice in writing given by either party to the other that [he][she][it] desires to terminate this Agreement

          (iii)   Immediately on the breach by the Fundraiser of any of the provisions of clause 2 of this Agreement or on the conviction of the Fundraiser of any criminal offence involving dishonesty

    5.2   On the termination of this Agreement the Fundraiser must hand over to the Charity forthwith any funds, documents or other property belonging to the Charity or in respect of which the copyright belongs to the Charity

6. REMUNERATION

    6.1   The Fundraiser shall be entitled to reimbursement of all reasonable out of pocket expenses incurred for the Project in accordance with the terms of this Agreement after production of all relevant receipts relating to those expenses and for the avoidance of doubt it is agreed that such expenses may include reasonable travelling, subsistence and hotel expenses

    6.2   The Fundraiser will be entitled to a fee of £. . . . per [day][hour] in respect of work which [he][she][it] certifies to have been carried out exclusively on the Project: provided that total fees in excess of £. . . . will not be payable under this sub-clause without the written approval of the Charity obtained before the additional work is undertaken.

6.3 All remuneration to the Fundraiser under this Agreement will be payable by cheque within 30 days of receipt of an invoice and supporting receipts and certificates from the Fundraiser. The Fundraiser is not entitled to retain on account of such remuneration any sums due to the Charity under clause 2 above

7. VARIATION

The terms of this Agreement, other than clause 2 and clause 6.3 above and this clause, may be varied in writing signed by both parties.

8. GENERAL

8.1 The Charity will use its best endeavours to co-operate with and assist the Fundraiser in carrying out the Project, and in particular will supply to the Fundraiser copies of such documents and such other materials belonging to the Charity as will better enable the Fundraiser to carry out the Project

8.2 If, in the Charity's opinion, the Project is successful, the Charity will authorise the Fundraiser to publish or disclose to other clients the Fundraiser's contribution to the Project

8.3 For ease of communication between the Charity and the Fundraiser the Charity will normally be represented by [specified officer] and the Fundraiser will normally be represented by [Name of individual] and all notices sent to or by either of those persons will be treated as notices to or from the Charity or the Fundraiser as the case may be

8.4 Whether or not this Agreement has been terminated, neither party will take legal proceedings for the enforcement of the terms of this Agreement or of any rights arising under it, without first having taken positive steps to resolve the matter by negotiation, mediation or other informal method of dispute resolution not involving publicity

[8.5 It is intended that this Agreement will be executed on the Charity's behalf by two of the trustees authorised by resolution under section 82 of the Charities Act 1993]

THIS AGREEMENT WAS EXECUTED BY THE CHARITY AND THE FUNDRAISER ON [DATE]

[Signatures for charity]

In the presence of

[Name and address of Witness]

[Signature of Fundraiser]

In the presence of

[Name and address of Witness]

7. Deed of Covenant

THIS DEED OF COVENANT made the [date] by
[Full name and address of supporter] ("the Donor")

WITNESSES as follows:

1.   The Donor covenants to pay to the [Name and address of Charity] [by monthly instalments of £. . . .] on the [date] in every [month][year] starting on [date of first payment] an annual sum which after deduction of income tax at the standard rate amounts to £. . . . for the term of 4 years from the date of the first payment

2.   This covenant will come to an end automatically on the death of the Donor at any time before the end of the term of 4 years

IN WITNESS whereof the Donor has executed this Deed

SIGNED AS A DEED by the Donor

[Signature of Donor]

In the presence of

[Name and address of witness – not a member of the Donor's family or a trustee or employee of the Charity]

Appendix B: Official Addresses

The Charity Commissioners

St Alban's House, 57–60 Haymarket, London SW1Y 4QX
Tel 071-210 4477

Woodfield House, Tangier, Taunton, Somerset TA1 4BL
Tel 0823 345000

Graeme House, Derby Square, Liverpool L2 7SB
Tel 051 227 3191

Inland Revenue (Claims Branch)

First Floor, St John's House, Merton Road, Bootle L69 9BB
Tel 051 922 6363

Treasury Solicitor's Department

Queen Anne's Chambers, 28 Broadway, London SW1H 9NN
Tel 071-210 3000

Home Office Voluntary Services Unit

50 Queen Anne's Gate, London SW1H 9AT
Tel 071-273 3000

Registrar of Companies

Companies House, Crown Way, Cardiff CF4 3UZ
Tel 0222 380801

Registrar of Friendly Societies

15 Marlborough Street, London W1V 1AF
Tel 071-437 9992

Department for Education

Sanctuary Building, Great Smith Street, London SW1P 3BT
Tel 071-925 5000

Housing Corporation

149 Tottenham Court Road, London W1P 0BN
Tel 071-387 9466

Church Commissioners

1 Millbank, London SW1P 3JZ
Tel 071-222 7010

Department of Health

Richmond House, 79 Whitehall, London SW1A 2NS
Tel 071 210 3000

Department of the Environment

2 Marsham Street, London SW1P 3EB
Tel 071-276 0900

For **Customs & Excise** and **DSS** enquiries, contact the local enquiry office.

Appendix C: Helpful Organisations

Almshouse Association

Billingbear Lodge, Wokingham, Berkshire RG11 5RU
Tel 0344 52922

Association of Charitable Foundations (ACF) (Grant-makers only)

High Holborn House, 52–54 High Holborn, London WC1V 6RL
Tel 071-404 1338

Centre for Dispute Resolution (CEDR) Charities Unit

100 Fetter Lane, London EC4A 1DD
Tel 071-430 1852/831 2852

Charities Aid Foundation (Gifts to charity, publications etc)

114 Southampton Row, London WC1B 5AA
Tel 071-831 7798

Charities Official Investment Fund

St Alphage House, 2 Fore Street, London EC2Y 5AQ
Tel 071-588 1815

Charity Appointments (Recruitment consultants)

3 Spital Yard, London E1 6AQ
Tel 071-247 4502

Charitybase (Accommodation for charities)

50 Westminster Bridge Road, London SE1 7QY
Tel 071-721 7650

Charity Finance Directors Group

Tanners Lane, Ilford, Essex
Tel 081-503 9217

Charity Forum (Training, PR, fundraising, management)

60 Laurel Avenue, Potters Bar, Hertfordshire EN6 2AB
Tel 0707 662448

Charity Recruitment (Recruitment consultants)

40 Rosebery Avenue, London EC1R 4RN
Tel 071-833 0770

Directory of Social Change (Training, publications)

169 Queen's Crescent, London NW5 4DS
Tel 071-284 4364/5/6; 071-284 3445

Institute of Charity Fundraising Managers (ICFM)

208 Market Towers, 1 Nine Elms Lane, London SW8 5NQ
Tel 071-627 3436/3508

Institute of Chartered Secretaries and Administrators (ICSA)
(Charities Group – training, publications)

16 Park Crescent, London W1N 4AH
Tel 071-580 4741

Joseph Rowntree Foundation (Publications, research)

The Homestead, 40 Water End, York YO3 6LP
Tel 0904 629241

London School of Economics (Centre for voluntary organisations)

Houghton Street, London WC2A 2AE
Tel 071-405 7686

National Council for Voluntary Organisations (NCVO) (Training, publications, advice)

Regent's Wharf, 8 All Saints Street, London N1 9RL
Tel 071-713 6161

National Federation of Community Organisations

8 Upper Street, London N1 0PQ
Tel 071-226 0189

National Federation of Housing Associations

175 Gray's Inn Road, London WC1X 8UE
Tel 071-278 6571

Rainbows & Unicorns (Training)

41 Temple Grange, Werrington, Peterborough PE4 5DN
Tel 0733 320613

South Bank University Business School (Course in charity finance)

103 Borough Road, London SE1 0AA
Tel 071-928 8989

Trustee Register (Finding trustees)

23 Peascod Street, Windsor, Berkshire SL4 1DE
Tel 0753 868277

NB   This list is not exhaustive; apologies to those inadvertently omitted.

Appendix D: Further Reading

Journals

Most 'umbrella' and specialist bodies publish their own Journal or Newsletter, eg *NCVO News*, *ACF Newsletter*, the *Almshouse Gazette*.

General charity journals include *Third Sector*, *Charity Magazine*, *Charities and Associations*, *Local Charity*.

More specialist journals: *NGO Finance*, *Charity Law and Practice Review*, *The Charity Finance Director's Handbook*, *Professional Fundraising*.

Short Books

There are numerous leaflets, booklets, reports and modestly priced books on particular aspects of charities published by the Charity Commissioners (eg *Starting a Charity*), NCVO (eg *On Trust* report), The Directory of Social Change (eg *School Fundraising* (Ann Mountfield)), Joseph Rowntree Foundation (eg *Trusts in Transition*) and others including several firms of solicitors.

Textbooks

NB Some textbooks are still in the process of being updated.

Sheridan and Keeton: *Modern Law of Charities* (Barry Rose, 1992)
Tudor: *Tudor on Charities* (Sweet & Maxwell, 1984)
Picarda: *Law and Practice Relating to Charities* (Butterworths, 1977)
Cracknell: *Charities, Law and Practice* (Longman, 1993)
Cairns: *Charities: Law and Practice* (Sweet & Maxwell, 1993)
Poole: *Education Law* (Sweet & Maxwell, 1988)
Alder and Handy: *Housing Association Law* (Sweet & Maxwell, 1991)
Dale: *The Law of the Parish Church* (Butterworths, 1989)
Vincent: *Charity Accounting & Taxation* (Butterworths, 1991)

Encyclopaedias and looseleaf works

Halsbury's Laws of England: (Charities title)
Butterworth's Encyclopaedia of Forms and Precedents:
(Charities, Sale of Land and Wills and Administration titles)

ICSA Charities Administration
Croner's Charities Manual
Tolley's Charities Manual

Europe

Nugent: *The Government and Politics of the European Community* (Macmillan, 1991)
Harvey: *Networking in Europe: a Guide to European Voluntary Organisations* (NCVO Publications, 1992)
NCVO: *Grants from Europe*

General interest books

Andrew Acland: *A Sudden Outbreak of Common Sense* (mediation)
Lloyd: *The Charity Business* (companies and charity) (John Murray, 1993)
Impey and Montague: *Running a Limited Company* second edition (Jordans, 1993)

Appendix E: Popular Misconceptions about Charity Law

There are a number of inaccurate ideas about charity law and the supervision of charities, some of which are mentioned below.

The Charity Commission

"The Charity Commissioners are all lawyers." No. There must be at least three and may be up to five Commissioners, two of whom must be solicitors or barristers.

"The Commissioners take all the decisions personally." No, most decisions are taken by Assistant Commissioners.

"The Official Custodian is a wizened gnome." No, she is a normal human being.

Registration

"A charity obtains charitable status by registration." No, an institution has or has not charitable status as soon as it is formed.

"A charity cannot obtain tax relief if it is not registered." No, the Inland Revenue, in granting relief from tax, operates independently of the register of charities.

"The Charity Commissioners will not register a new charity which performs the same function as an existing charity." No, there is no power to do this.

"If the Charity Commissioners find that a charity has been mismanaged they will remove it from the register or take away its charitable status." No, in that situation they may pursue the trustees for breach of trust, take steps to safeguard the assets and ensure that they are used for charitable purposes.

Complaints

"The Commissioners will investigate any complaint against a charity." No, anonymous or unfounded complaints are not usually investigated.

"If a charity is under investigation there must be something wrong with its administration." No, many investigations do not result in that conclusion.

"A question about a particular charity may be asked in Parliament'. Normally, only general questions will be answered.

Charitable Purposes

"Charities must benefit the poor." No, but charities should not exclude the poor.

"Charities must be non-profit-making." No, many charities need to make a profit (or surplus) to survive. Charities may not distribute profits to members, however.

Trusteeship

"An ex officio trustee need not take part in the running of the charity." No, he or she is equally responsible with the rest of the trustees.

"An ex officio trustee should always be the Chairman." No, normally it is for the trustees to choose the Chairman from time to time.

"A co-opted trustee has no vote." No, unless there is a specific provision in the governing instrument to the contrary, a trustee who has been co-opted (ie appointed by the trustee body) has the same voting power as any other trustee.

"A trustee appointed by an outside body represents that body at trustee meetings." No, the sole duty of any trustee is to act in the interests of the charity.

"A trustee appointed by an outside body may be removed by that body." No, not unless there is an express power of removal in the charity's governing instrument.

"A trustee appointed by an outside body must be a member of that body." No, it is immaterial unless the governing instrument specifically provides for him or her to be a member.

"A trustee who carries out work for a charity can be paid for it." No, except in special cases where the governing instrument allows payment, or the Charity Commissioners give their approval (in advance), trustees may not be paid anything more than their expenses, whatever work they do for the charity.

"Trustees appointed by local authorities are entitled to an attendance allowance for attending meetings of the trustees." No.

"Trustees are entitled to bump up their expenses." No, they are only permitted to be reimbursed their actual out-of-pocket expenses, and only so long as these are reasonable.

Expenditure

"It is wrong for charities to spend money on administration." No, obviously they should spend whatever is necessary to run the charity efficiently and properly. This varies according to the type of charity concerned.

"It is wrong for charities to build up reserves." No, for some charities it is essential to do this in order to manage the charity well and to plan ahead. If an excessive amount is saved, however, the trustees will need to reconsider their policy on grant-making or fundraising.

"Charities should not spend money which has been given to them on fundraising." No, very often initial expenditure is required in order to raise funds effectively. On the other hand, the charity must watch the return on its initial expenditure, and should not involve itself in fundraising for its own sake.

Appendix F: Names to Avoid

The Charities (Misleading Names) Regulations 1992 contain a list of words which trustees would do well to avoid using in the title to their charity, since the Commissioners may require the name to be altered on the ground that the public might otherwise be misled. The list of specified words is as follows:

Technical terms (appropriate only if legally accurate):

Bank, Building Society, Co-operative, Friendly Society, Industrial & Provident Society, Grant-Maintained, Polytechnic, School, Trade Union, University.

Words with governmental or geographical connotations (appropriate only if correctly describing the charity's area of operation or class of beneficiaries):

British, England, English, Europe, European, Great Britain, Great British, International, Ireland, Irish, National, Nationwide, Northern Ireland, Northern Irish, Scotland, Scottish, United Kingdom, Wales, Welsh.

Words which suggest an official connection or connection with a substantial organisation (usually inappropriate, except in the case of "Church" in a religious context):

Assurance, Authority, Benevolent, Church, Official, Registered.

Words suggesting a Royal connection (rarely appropriate, and then permission may be required):

Her Majesty, His Majesty, King, Prince, Princess, Queen, Royal, Royale, Royalty, Windsor.

Charities may also be required to alter names which are too like the name of another charity, or which are offensive, although the author is unaware of any charity attempting to adopt a name in the last category.

Index